D0429917

READ BETWEEN THE LINES

From the Diary of a Teenage Mom

JENELLE EVANS
with Tonia Brown

Post Hill
PRESS

A POST HILL PRESS BOOK

Read Between the Lines:
From the Diary of a Teenage Mom
© 2017 by Jenelle Evans
All Rights Reserved

ISBN: 978-1-68261-403-7
ISBN (eBook): 978-1-68261-404-4

Cover photograph by David Eason
Interior Design and Production by Greg Johnson

Post Hill Press
New York • Nashville
posthillpress.com

Published in the United States of America

Contents

Turning the Pages

Looking back on your past is easy when you've spent a large part of it on camera. Everyone thinks they know you because they see so much of your life on the small screen. You come into the viewer's living room, give them a glimpse into your world, and folks walk away thinking they understand how you got from point A to point pregnant. The truth is always more complicated than a camera can capture. But the truth is also hard for us to pin down because memory is a funny thing. You think you remember something so clearly, only to doubt yourself later on when you think about it again.

Keeping a diary helps with these little details.

While moving things around to get ready for our new house, I rediscovered my old teenage diaries. Three little books, all as different as the years recorded inside. I was struck by the sight of them, and remembered that I began writing things down as a way to help me deal with my crazy life. An overbearing mother. A pair of impulsive siblings. A dad that I barely knew. My diary gave me an understanding audience. One that didn't judge me. One that kept all of my secrets. One that just let me be me.

As I poured over the small pages, I saw the path of my life written in adorable, childish scribbles. The more I read, the more I wondered if others would like to read them. Yes. The answer was yes, I think others would like to read them. After all, I had an audience for my teenage years. Why not gather an audience for my childhood? Paint a complete picture that is Jenelle.

I am not saying these stories explain everything about me. It won't be an outline of *this is to blame for my mistakes*, or *that is the fault for all of my problems*. What I hope to share is the journey of my youth. Of how I got from point A to point pregnant, and beyond.

If life is about the journey and not the destination, then this book is a map of my voyage so far. I hope you can find something worthy in the trip while I try to rediscover the innocence of my youth.

The F Word

Before we get into the pages of my diaries, I want to talk about the F word.

No, not that one. If you've ever heard me talk, you know I say that one enough as it is.

In this case, I am talking about family. Family is a funny thing, you know? Here are a group of people you are tied to through something as thick as blood, but in most cases these are the last people in the world you would choose to have as friends. Now I know there are families out there who are all happy-go-lucky and hardly ever argue. (Or at least they would like for you to think that.) I know that some families get a long great, most of the time, and actually look forward to holidays and other gatherings. There are some families who struggle to get along, those who come together in times of trouble, but overall keep to themselves.

Then there was my family.

A lot of folks think they have the worst family, or wished they had a different family, or belonged to someone else's family. Don't get me wrong. I don't believe I have the worst relatives in the history of ever. And I am not so naïve that I believe there is such a thing as a perfect family. I just wished there had been more *family* to ours. We never had fun vacations or cozy holidays. There wasn't a gathering that didn't end in a screaming match. Sure, we had our moments, those rare occasions when everything clicked and for a shining moment everyone was tolerable. Of course, it never lasted, and we would slip right back into those icy waters of indifference or sometimes pure hatred.

Our family was originally from Scranton, Pennsylvania. It's a nice enough town, but I never cared for it. I never fit in at school. I never made many friends. I just didn't like it there. In fact, the first half of my earliest diary is missing; torn away and long gone. That's right, I hated my time in Scranton so much, I ripped out my diary entries and threw them away! My first entry after that was about how much I hated my life in Pennsylvania. Well, that and how I was grounded alongside my brother. Which brings us back to the F word.

Family.

I have one sister, Ashleigh, and one brother, Colin. I will talk more about them later, and believe me, there is lots to talk about. Most of you know my mother Barbara from her time on television with me. She and I have a complicated

4

history, and while I love her, we don't have that special mother-daughter bond I hear other's talk so much about. I wished we could be closer to one another, but there is so much standing between us I don't think we will ever get there. For all the distance between my mother and myself, there is twice the length between my dad and me.

Robert Evans was only in my life for a little while. For that short and glorious time, I was daddy's little girl. I loved and admired him. I still do in some small way. Without warning everything changed, and my dad cut himself out of my life. Even now, as a grown woman, we don't talk. Maybe one day that will change. Maybe one day we can find one another, get to know each other, and he can finally be my *father*. Until then, he is just my biological dad. All I have of him are memories; some good, some bad, and some heartbreaking. Of course, I have the horrible stories my mother tells me about him. There are also the uncomfortable claims my siblings have made about him. (More on that later.)

Folks tell me I have a romanticized view of my dad as a cool, fun-loving guy. I suppose that's because it was the only part of him I got to see. I only have my memories to go on, and in my mind, he was laid back and calm compared to the rest of the family. My mother was always fussing and arguing with me, but my dad was much calmer. He was musically inclined, which I always thought was fun. He was an awesome singer and a musician. He liked to drive around with all of the windows down, the radio blasting, and the two of us singing at the top of our lungs. Once he even played in a band with a famous actor!

But my dad, the rock star? Not so much. Later, my mother explained he wasn't a rock star husband. He worked at a recording studio for a number of years, but playing music never paid the family's bills. He had some other habits like carousing and hanging out with his friends instead of staying home that made her mad too. Yeah, my mother used to give him hell for every little thing he did, but looking back on it now, I have to wonder if maybe she was just lashing out at him because of his misplaced sense of priorities. She never thought he put his family first, at least that's what I always got from her.

Or maybe there were things there I never got.

To a little girl that never saw the adult side of him, my dad seemed like a fun-loving kind of guy. To be fair to my mother, I was young when he still lived in the house, and never knew what went on when they were alone. Having been in and out of my own troubled relationships, I can only guess at what their marriage was like. It was rocky enough not to last, and that says enough on its own, I suppose. I wished I had paid enough attention at the time, so I could watch for the same signs in my own life.

My mother did share one story with me, however. She explained once that dad fell down a full flight of stairs, while holding a three-year-old. Guess who was that three-year-old little girl? Right. Me! According to my mother, I woke up with a nightmare one night and wandered the house until I ended up downstairs with him. He rocked me to sleep and then he tried to carry me back upstairs. When he reached the top step, he lost his footing and fell all the way back down, with me still in his arms. I turned out to be okay, but that was the final nail in the coffin as far as mom was concerned. It was shortly after that my mother kicked him out.

He went to live with his own mother when Barbara threw him out. My mother filed for divorce soon after, and by October 13 of '94, they were officially done. Ten years of marriage gone thanks to bad habits and bad attitude. We still got to see our dad because they shared custody, and through these visits I sort of got to know my old man. I still remember those long drives with the radio blasting and all of us singing along. I would go to our grandmother's house, his mom, and watch him record music onto her computer. He showed me how to edit music, and eventually got me my first digital camera. He encouraged me to make films and this lead to my desire to pursue a career in film editing. I remember him being supportive and encouraging. I guess people can have all sorts of sides. The ones they show you, and the ones they keep for other people.

I never thought those days would end. Then they did. All of a sudden it was over. He was out of our lives just like that. You would think it was the big move from Pennsylvania to North Carolina that did it, but no. My dad stepped out of my life before that. I still don't understand what really happened.

My mother began dating again a while after the divorce, and after a few hit and misses she eventually met Mike. He became her long-time boyfriend. Mike's a good guy, and I didn't mind calling him my step dad. During the time they spent together he was supportive of my mom, and she loved him. I am glad she had someone she could depend on for a little while since my dad was such a letdown to her. They split eventually, with him moving back to Pennsylvania and them selling our old house in North Carolina. It seems like none of the relationships in my life last very long, even the ones I am not a part of.

Mike also played a weird part in the last time I saw my dad.

The last memory I have of seeing Robert Evans was waiting for him to come and pick my siblings and me up for our weekend stay. We were sitting on the porch waiting patiently, Mike standing with us, when our dad's car pulled down the road. Dad slowed down, looked right at all of us sitting there, then pulled away as if he didn't know any of us.

After that, we never saw him again. He never returned to get us. Never picked us up for another visit. That was that. I always wondered if it because he saw mom's new boyfriend with us. Did he think Mike was filling the role of our father?

I never got to find out because I only talked to him one more time after that.

After we relocated to North Carolina, I walked in on a phone call between him and my mother. I have no idea how often they talked or if that was the only time. I lingered, wanting to hear their discussion, and waiting to see if I could get a chance to talk to him.

The conversation must have gotten around to his kids, because she paused and looked at me while saying, "She doesn't want to talk to you."

I said, "Um, yes I do."

She begrudgingly handed me the phone.

I immediately asked him where he had been.

"Home," he said, meaning my grandmother's in Scranton. "How are you?"

I wanted to talk to him, to tell him how much I missed him and how I wished he was here with us in North Carolina. I wanted to tell him about the friends I had made since the move, and how Ashleigh and Colin weren't any less annoying and how mom still barked all of the time about everything we did. Above all else, I wanted to know why he left us on the porch that day. Why did he just drive by? Turned out I couldn't bring myself to say any of this.

All I could manage to say was, "I'm good. When are you coming for a visit?"

I never heard his answer. As soon as the words were out of my mouth, my mother snatched the phone away from me. She grumbled something into the phone about setting up visits but that he would have to come to North Carolina. They talked for a bit longer, but I never got another chance to talk to him that day. Or ever again.

To this day, I don't know if my mother forced him out of our lives or if he just didn't want us anymore. I can't help but think it was a bit of both. On the one hand, I could tell our mother had done everything she could to cut our dad out of our lives. On the other, he never made much of an effort to resist her. It wasn't like he fought her in court for custody. What little visitation he was awarded he gave up on without a word. I still love him, but deep down I think I will always be that heartbroken little girl waiting on the porch for her daddy to come and pick her up.

I would like to think my dad is a great but misunderstood man. I would like to, but he cut me out of his life when I was eleven. It's hard to draw an opinion of a man who I feel gave up on me...and life in general.

As for my siblings, there's a whole different set of stories. I know why they call it sibling rivalry because I sure fought with my brother and sister a lot. Yet my relationship trouble with the pair of them goes far beyond just healthy competition or natural disagreements. There was always something inherently broken in our relationship. I never got along much with either of them, unless we were up to no good. When we were sneaking around or lying to our mother or generally being little brats, we got along great. But on a supportive, nurturing level, we failed. I have no memories of my older sister comforting me in times of trouble, or my older brother sticking up for me. Most of my memories with my siblings are breaking things or being grounded or just my mother screaming at us for something we did or didn't do.

Ashleigh is older than both of us, and she made sure we remembered it. She was snobby and bitchy, and had no time for either Colin or me. I only wanted to hang out with my cool older sister, but no. Between her words and actions, she pushed me away as hard as she could. She had her friends and her social life, she didn't need a younger sister dragging her down. I made a few entries about getting into fights with her. Not just screaming matches either. Actual fistfights. I am not sure who won more often, her or me. I just remember getting into it on a near daily basis with her over every little thing.

Colin is a year younger than Ashleigh. He and I got along better than either of us did with our sister. I have always been more of a tomboy anyways, and Colin liked to do the things I liked to do. Ride bikes. Play outside. Find trouble and get as deep as we could into it. Even though I was a few years younger than him, he let me hang out with him and his friends. I think maybe this is when I started preferring guy friends over girlfriends. He often had outbursts of rage, and I was usually the person who could calm him down. It took some time for me to realize those outbursts were more than just a phase he was going through. He had some serious problems going on inside of his head.

Growing up I spent a lot of time with my brother, so when he got agitated, I had more patience for him. Not so much for my sister. She was a ball of stress I never really understood. To be fair, all three of us suffer from various emotional problems. Personally, I have to deal with layers of PTSD, anxiety, and other stress factors. My siblings have different issues that I can't even begin to explain here.

My sister started showing signs of stressing out at a very young age. Even at six she was a stressed-out kid. What a six-year-old has to stress out about, I don't know, but she did. Somewhere around fifth grade my sister's grades started to slip. She was never a straight-A student, but it got so bad she had to repeat the fifth grade. This meant she had to go to the same class with Colin. This embarrassed her and of course made her stress levels far worse. She was easy to make mad, which I managed to do all of the time. It wasn't just me, however. She fought with everyone in her life, friends and family. After she repeated the fifth grade, Ashleigh slid deeper into a dark place. She went through a Goth phase, with all black clothes and stuff like that.

She also dabbled in witchcraft and other weird stuff. She became known around school for her unusual behavior, and stress issues. Which spilled over into my life in a way she couldn't control, but I suffered for.

Everyone remembered or knew of my older sister, and assumed I was exactly like her. As a result, I didn't make friends as easily. Everyone thought they knew how I was going to be, so they didn't take the time to get to know me. We lived in a small town and went to a small school. Even the teachers thought they knew what to expect from me based on their experience with her. It might have been selfish of me at the time, but I really hated her for it. I felt like I couldn't get past the idea of her. Like I was set up to fail.

All of that changed when we moved to North Carolina. It was a fresh start for me. Nobody knew my sister so they didn't have a preconceived notion of how I should act. I could make my own path without the history of her or my brother's behavior changing it. No one knew anything about my strange sister or violent brother. I had a fresh piece of paper to write on. For once, I could set my own expectations.

Things did change for me. I found new purpose and tried things I never thought I would do before in Scranton. I became a cheerleader, got a chance to do some modeling, and more importantly I made tons of new friends. I was happy for the first time in Oak Island. I never cared if I saw the likes of Pennsylvania ever again. My sister? Not so much.

When I say everything changed, I meant everything. Ashleigh didn't want to move to North Carolina. She pitched a fit when she found out we were leaving Pennsylvania. I understand why. Moving isn't easy for a family. Picking up your life and relocating it is rough on adults, but it's worse on the kids. She had friends and history within our old territory. She was already fifteen and well established in our little community, even if it was as a strange teenager. My sister had a life in Scranton, and now she had to abandon all of it and start over again. She was more than just upset about the move. She was pissed off about it.

She ranted and raved, screaming at my mom and her new boyfriend (Mike) about how they were ruining her life. My sister put on an epic display of spoiled brathood with her outburst. It was almost as violent as my brother got on occasion. She didn't want to go and there was nothing that was going to change her mind. We couldn't have been more different about our old home. Whereas I ripped up my old diary entries and threw them out because I hated my life there, she jumped up and down screaming about never wanting to leave the place.

In the end, she lost the fight and the battle. We moved to North Carolina and never went back to Pennsylvania. She probably counts this as one of the points her life was ruined. She didn't recover well from the move. Couldn't make friends as easily as she did in Scranton. Never became as popular as she was back in our old home. She continued her therapy visits and I am sure she had lots and lots to talk about in her now forever-changed life.

These days Ashleigh lives in a house near our mom. At one point, she married a marine and had a kid. That marriage didn't last long. She went out with another guy for a while after her divorce, but that didn't last long either. Later she ended up having a second kid with her ex-husband's best friend. I know, right? Through all of this she still seems so unsatisfied. My sister has never seemed happy to me. I feel bad for her. I don't think I have ever seen her truly happy. I don't know if she ever will be. I wish her all the happiness in the world, but I don't know if she has it in her to be a happy person. Some people live through misery. They are only satisfied when everything, and everyone, around them are broken.

My brother, as much as I enjoyed spending time with him, wasn't much better in the broken department. Where my sister was well known for being unstable and weird, he was known for his outbursts and violent tendencies. There were lots of times in our childhood where he would suffer an emotional break, and the result was like a bomb going off. He would get really violent, lashing out with words and fists. More than once he lashed out at his own family. I remember many times when I was frightened by his outbursts. I was able to handle most of his actions, but sometimes he was far too out of control for even me to reel him in.

Then there was the day he accidentally set the house on fire.

It was an afternoon in late July of 2000. My mom and my sister and me were downstairs watching a horror movie when Colin came running down the stairs from the attic. He shouted, waving his arms and hollering almost incoherently. It took us a few moments of confusion to figure out what in the hell he was going on about. I think I smelled the smoke first. Colin had started a fire in the attic and it was quickly spreading to the rest of the house.

Later we learned he set a toy car alight, then tossed it onto his bed, which then caught the entire attic on fire. Keep in mind he wasn't a two- or three-year-old toying with matches. This was a nine-year-old boy deliberately setting fire to his toys. God only knows how long the fire was burning before he finally came and told us what he had done.

Even though I was only six, my mother grabbed me by the shoulders and told me to run to the neighbor's house and get them to call the fire department. I think that says a lot about the two of them; rather than get either of my older siblings to call for help she sent the six-year-old to do it. After that, she yelled at all of us to get out. Smart woman.

Again, she may have her faults, she didn't want us stay in the house to call for help. She wanted her children out of the burning building so they could stay safe.

I followed her instructions and ran as fast I could to the next house. I explained in a panic rush to the neighbors what was going on, then ran back to the house to make sure our mom was okay. She stayed inside for a long time. Longer than was safe for anyone to be in a burning house. She was trying to save our home, trying to fight the now raging fire. She failed. By the time the fire truck arrived, a good portion of our house had burned to the ground. Mother was devastated.

She wasn't the only one. All of our lives were ruined by the fire. Not just our earthly possessions were consumed. Part of our childhood died in those flames too. My mother was between boyfriends at the time, and had no one else she could call for help. She had to rely on our dad to come and pick us up and take care of us so she could handle things for the rest of the day. Our dad did as asked, but later when she was supposed to return and get us, she didn't show. We got word that she had spent the evening out with some friends to blow off some steam over the whole affair.

Once again, a parental unit didn't want us around. Surprise, surprise.

Thankfully our mother was a well-prepared woman. She carried home owner's insurance which paid for not only repairs but also for all of our ruined possessions and housing for the duration of the repairs. The four of us ended up spending about six months in a local motel while they fixed the house. We got all new stuff, which was nice, but again, the event was harrowing and traumatic. It was a breaking point for our mother concerning her son's behavior. Until then she had been sending him to therapy and keeping him on medication for his various conditions. His outbursts were dealt with incident by incident. This, however, was too much for all of us.

Colin ended up in a special group home in Texas for nearly two years. I don't blame my mother for sending him away like that. It is a hard decision, yet I would've done the same. He still lives in a special group home. Turns out, not only does Colin have the family issue of anxiety, he is also developmentally challenged. Which I guess explains a lot about his whole life. What normal kid goes from killing ants with a magnifying glass to setting the family house on fire? My mother had to make some more hard choices when it came to what was best for him, and one of those was placing him in a permanent group home where he could get the kind of care he needs.

I suppose this brings me back around to my mother. Wow, that is a long, complicated subject. For those of you who have watched the show, it is no secret that I have a terribly complicated relationship with my mother. From the exchanges we have made on camera you would think we have never gotten along. Funny thing is, at one point we did get along... sort of. Once upon a time, out of the three of us, I was the child she yelled at the least. That was enough to make me the favorite. She once told me I was her normal kid, because I didn't need therapy or medication. (Yet!) Hey, I said we weren't your usual family, didn't I?

My mom married my dad in April of '84. They stayed married for ten years. Ten long years, according to her. I don't think my father started out the marriage that way. I think maybe the responsibility of married life just weighed down on him too much. I can't say that for sure, of course. Either way, the course of things lead to their divorce, and Barbara became a single mom of three kids. She had a tough job.

She made it work. She had to become both the mom and the dad, and somewhere in there I lost touch with her. She had to crack down on us twice as hard because she didn't have someone else to share the burden of discipline with her. My mother developed into a harsher, colder version of herself. She was already hard on us. After dad left, she began to scrutinize everything we did. I would like to say I reacted to it with grace and maturity. Obviously, I did not. I was just a kid, and I wanted to push her as hard as she pushed me. Teenagers test their parents, and since she was my only one, she got twice the dosage. If she yelled, I yelled. If she shoved, I shoved. Screaming matches became the norm for all of us. There was never a quiet moment in the house again.

After dad moved out and she divorced him, my mother was alone for a while. She had some friends and family that lived close, but she stayed off the dating market for a time. As a fresh divorcee, she was probably giving those old wounds time to heal. Eventually she began dating again, and when she did, she wasn't shy about introducing us to her new boyfriend. She never hid it from us or kept it separate from us. Some of her boyfriends were okay. Just normal guys doing their best to find a partner they could settle down with. But some... some guys weren't the best choices in men. I think now I can see where I got my lousy choice in men!

One boyfriend in particular we called Cookie. He had a daughter about Ashleigh's age. I learned how to cuss from the pair of them. They would teach me certain words, which I had no idea what they meant, and then get me to say them in front of my mother. Of course, this would get me in trouble. Cookie and his daughter would just laugh and laugh about it. Mom didn't think it was very funny. He wasn't around for long.

Mom met Mike a year or so before we moved to North Carolina. He was her first longstanding relationship since our father moved out. I got to where I would call him my stepdad, even though he never married mom or adopted us. I liked him and I still do, but that too didn't last. A few years ago, he split up with my mom and moved out. I guess nothing lasts forever. Children grow up, love fades, people move on.

Again, if you watched the show, you know how I fell into the trap of signing over the custody of my son Jace. I thought I was doing it so I could get my life back on track and regain custody of my son. I made a lot of easy missteps and stupid mistakes, but I tried my hardest to do right by him. In the end, it didn't matter. The courts awarded her full custody and she has retained rights ever since. It has been a nightmarish battle to get him back into my home and arms. Even though I have other children who are doing perfectly fine, they won't give him back to me. It hurts my heart when I think about it. And I think about it every day. I could fill this book with descriptions of my heartache, but let me stop before I get started. This book isn't about the Jenelle of today. This book is about the Jenelle of years ago.

Starting on Sunday, February 15, 2004.

The Kitten Diary

The Kitten Diary is the first of three in my small collection of memories. It's a thin, pink journal featuring a photograph of an adorable ginger kitten asleep in a set of white sheets. It's almost too perfect for a preteen girl to record her deepest secrets. It, like the other two diaries, is not as filled with entries as I hoped it would be. It is filled with scribbles and scratches. Lots of things scrawled on the front and the inside cover. Lots of things crossed out as well. It's a mess, kind of like my childhood.

This one is the shortest of the three, for two reasons. One, as I said before, I tore out a small handful of pages and threw them away. I must've gotten rid of them when I discovered I was moving to North Carolina. Who knows what really happened. Maybe one of my friends made me mad and I threw them away out of spite. Maybe there was something written in those pages better left forgotten.

The second reason this one is so short will become apparent as we go along.

The Kitten Diary is short. There are only five entries in this one, but it's a pretty good reflection of my last days in Pennsylvania. The first entry is several pages, and is one of the longer entries across the three diaries.

Feburary 15, 2004, Sunday.
Hello,
I didn't have a good
weekend. Colin flipped out
and Judy got involved.
She started to scream
at ME! Now Ashleigh
didn't even know what
happened and she
blamed everything on
me! So now me and
Colin are grounded
all week until Saturday
when we leave to go
to NC for another
week. I'm going out
with this kid named
David. I saw a pic of
David's brother, and IS
HE HOOOTTT!!! → ☀

* My friend, Mary,
On the other hand, her
father hates me, and
she is also grounded
at her mother's house,
until 4th quater! I
only like her between
50% and 60%. Because
she doesn't talk to me
at all at school but
then she called me
yesterday to say
Happy Valentine's Day.
But I thought Why
didn't you call me at
All?. Well Kate is mad
at me. But I don't
care, because I'm So
happy that I'm moving
to NC. I know that

it's terrible to say. But
also, I hate all my
friends! Expect Lisa,
Lisa is the only one
who is nice to me and
Cares about me and
she is the only one
I'm going to miss 100%.
And I'll just invite her
to NC and no one else.
Because it seems everyone
hates me. ~~xx~~ ~~xxx~~ Mary
wanted to go out with
David best friend. And
she never saw him! She
is such a little slut! And
I don't know what David
looks like but I knew
him since... Last Decem,
ber! And Mary ⟶ ✳

*never saw his best friend. Well I'll tell you what happens later. OK? See Ya! TTYT or Later!

Love,
Jenelle
Lauren
Madalynn
Evans

P.S. I'm getting my braces off the 2nd week of March! PARTY OVA HERE, Whoa, Whoa!

LOL

I was twelve years old at the time, and pretty expressive about my troubles at home. As you can see, I wasn't happy in Pennsylvania. Not happy with my home life. Not happy with my friends. Not happy with myself.

The first few lines are about an argument I had with Colin at our neighbor's house. He was an elderly neighbor and friend of our family, in his 70s or so. He was kind of like a grandfather to me. We would go over to his house and spend time with him, playing games and just hanging out with him. Judy was a friend of his that stayed with him sometimes. She wasn't as nice as he was. Whereas he enjoyed our company, Judy didn't like when we came over.

This particular day, Colin and I got into a fuss about something. Judy stuck her nose in the middle of it and started screaming at the pair of us about it. Then Ashleigh found out from Judy screaming, and of course she went running to mother about it. She told mom about our argument and mom immediately grounded Colin and me. No chance to defend ourselves or find out what it was all about. Just on our sister's word, we got grounded for a week. Funny thing is, I don't remember now what it was all about! It must've been important to me at the time, but here, almost thirteen years later, I can't recall what started it all.

Reading back on the entry makes me feel twelve all over again. The preteen angst and anger I had for my family is still there inside of me. It rears its ugly head every once in a while, and I know it's never going to go away. I hear stories about other siblings that leave me jealous. About brothers and sisters that do not get along very well, but they always joined up when it came to their parents. Cussing each other out was one thing. Running to mom and telling her everything so you can keep on her good side is a whole different, shitty move.

This argument happened a week or so before we were scheduled for a vacation in North Carolina at my aunt's beach house. My mother already had a yen to move and had already started looking for houses on the coast. By April we would move down there for good. Mike, her boyfriend, found work down there and moved ahead of us. We packed up and met him a few months later. I couldn't wait. This and the next entry reiterate how glad I was to leave Pennsylvania far behind me. I would be glad to see it in the rearview mirror for good.

Mary was a neighbor of mine in my old Pennsylvania neighborhood. We were pretty good friends but her father didn't like me very much. He really didn't want us hanging out at all. Mary used to get into trouble a lot just for spending time with me. A simple thing like walking to the park would make him mad at her. Damn! He was even stricter than my mom, and you guys that watch the show know that's saying a lot.

I remember it had snowed and all of us neighborhood kids were going to go sledding. We stopped to pick up Mary, but she couldn't come with us. Her dad said she couldn't go sledding because she didn't have snow pants. She couldn't even just come and hang out. We talked him into letting her come with us, on the rule that she didn't sled. She could watch, nothing more. I was mad because she couldn't sled just because of a pair of stupid pants.

So, I lent her a pair.

We may have sort have hid that part from her dad. Mary was really excited about it. I was too. I was so happy to see my friend enjoying herself. I find I have a tendency to ride other people's emotions, like some uninvited passenger on an uncontrollable rollercoaster. When they are up, I am up. When they are down, I hit rock bottom too. Seeing Mary enjoying herself made me feel good. All of that came to an abrupt end when she nearly broke her leg.

She came down the hill too fast and crashed into a bush. She was okay, but her dad got so mad about it. He grounded her once again and she went to stay with her mom. Her parents were divorced, like so many are these days. She split her life between her mom and her dad, and her punishment followed her around too. I was sort of jealous that her dad stayed in her life, even if he seemed to be mad at her most of the time. At least he cared enough to be concerned about her.

I was hung up on a kid named David, who I met through Mary. David and I talked online at first, through AOL messenger and other chat tools. This was back before we all had phones and could text each other. Most of our relationship was virtual, but eventually we met in person at the Boys and Girls club. He was nice and sweet. I don't talk about him much in the entry because there wasn't much to talk about. We talked online, met a few times in person, held hands. You know, stuff that twelve-year-olds do.

Two other girls I mention here are Kate and Lisa. They were best buds together, but also friends of mine. Kate was a little stuck up, and always wanted to do things her way. Lisa, on the other hand, was the nicest girl I knew. I really liked her because I could tell she liked me for me. She didn't expect anything from me. I have only had a few people like that in my life. Folks who are just glad to know me, and don't want anything else.

I was pretty pleased to be moving to North Carolina and away from the stigma of my family reputation. The few friends I did have, I didn't think I would miss. Of course, I missed some of them, but not all. I said at the time Lisa was the only one I was going to miss one hundred percent. I think I missed Mary most of all, and will later mention this in a diary entry.

Speaking of Mary, the last part of the entry is about how she wanted to go out with David's best friend, even though she had never seen him before. I even called her a little slut! Wow! Kids can be cruel, even to those they love the most. I think I was probably fussy because I thought I had taken the time to make a real relationship with David and she just wanted to say she was dating someone she hadn't even laid eyes on. Who knows? When you're twelve, you think everything is so damned dramatic.

The PS here is cute. I had braces at the time and was ready to get them off. It was kind of an important countdown for me. Again, the things a twelve-year-old thinks matters. Your world is all boys and clothes and getting your braces off. Life was easy and simple, even if I hated where I was.

Feburary 16, 2004, Monday

Hello,

I have no school today because it's President's Day. Today my mom lead me some slack and let me only upstairs and downstairs, for being grounded. But anyways me and my brother, Colin, took my cat, Molly, and threw him behind my chair, but Molly caught on to the plug and broke my grandmother's lamp! But we told my mom that Molly was just laying on the chair and fell behind it and broke ☀

—>

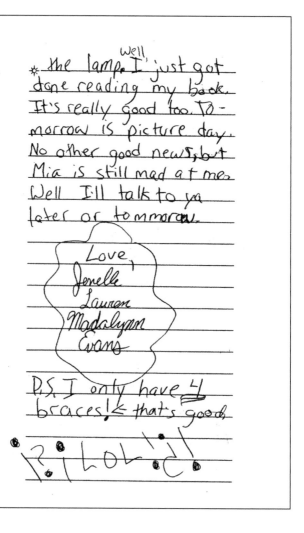

* the lamp. *well,* I just got done reading my book. It's really good too. Tomorrow is picture day. No other good news, but Mia is still mad at me. Well I'll talk to ya later or tommorow.

Love,
Jenelle
Lauren
Madalynn
Evans

P.S. I only have 4 braces! ← that's good

? LOL

So this was a day after the first entry. I was still grounded though my mother let up on me a little bit. She seemed to do that, run hot and cold on punishment. She would ground me for life one day, then the next I was allowed to watch television. The next I could go outside and play. The next I was off the hook. Of course, I always seemed to be grounded in the next week for life again, so it never really mattered. If my mother was a judge, she would have handed down a life sentence to me ten times over by the time I was sixteen.

Upon first reading this entry, I am sure some of you are worried about my cat Molly. I want to point out that the diary makes it sound a lot worse than it was. Colin wasn't throwing her around like a crazy person. He could get violent with us, but he wasn't trying to hurt Molly. He had heard that a cat always landed on its feet from any height.

He asked me if I had ever heard of this. I told him that I had. He asked if we should test it out. I said maybe, but I wasn't sure. Before I knew it, he snapped up Molly and tossed her to the floor. She ended up behind my chair, while Colin watched to see if she really landed on her feet. Again, he didn't fling her hard or throw her hard.

Molly caught the lamp cord and pulled my mother's stained glass lamp off of the end table. The lamp fell to the floor with a shattering crash and at once Colin and I knew we were in deep crap. That lamp was an antique my mother had gotten from her mother. A family heirloom, I believe it is called. Well, it was nothing but a pile of glass by the time we got done with it. It was an accident, sure, but an accident we caused and would surely get grounded for.

My mother came running, shocked to find her priceless lamp in shards. Of course, she immediately turned to us and demanded to know what happened. I could've pointed my finger at my brother. Better still, he could've blamed me. But we didn't. Instead, I explained how Molly was just lying on the chair and rolled over and fell off. She got caught in the cord when she slipped off the chair and took the lamp to the floor with her.

My brother caught onto my story and agreed. Yup. That's what happened, ma.

It was a beautiful thing. I know it might seem silly to dwell on this tale with such fondness, but it proves a point. One entry earlier, Ashleigh went running straight to mom and blabbed all about Colin and me. But when my brother and I got into trouble, we stuck up for each other. When the going got tough, and mom was ready to lay out some punishment, we stuck together and ended up getting away with it. Again, it was really just an accident to begin with, but our mother wasn't the kind of person to suffer even accidents lightly.

The rest of the entry is about my accelerated reading course. I've always been in advanced classes, and eventually

I would take early college courses during high school. I loved to read, so seeing that part of the entry isn't a surprise.

There's another PS about my braces. Just a kid counting the days until they came off!

Heyy,

⬤ I'm here in my new room in Oak Island N.C. I'm so happy I moved here because I'm sooo popular! Also I have tons of friends. Including Vicky and Tammy! I can't really decide who I like better, Tammy or Vicky There my top 2 bffe's! And as soon as I got here I got a boyfriend named Jack, I got my braces off that I had. And I'm a Cougar Cheerleader! O Yea. O Yea, about ＊

⁎ Jack   I really truely thinks I'll marry him someday, Because we're hooked on each other 100%. But I just told David on the internet that I'll go out with him when I knew I was going out with Jack. Dam! I'm so p.o.'ed with myself. Today me and my friend Andy got his Carma and recorded me and him jumping off his jump! It was anwsome! Well I'll TTYL!

♡ ⟶

Jenelle
Lauren
Madalynn
Evans

J. L. M. E.

While this one isn't dated, I can safely say it is from around August of 2004.

The first thing you will notice here is the huge jump in time. This is a pattern I will follow for my other diary entries too. I would let a few months pass between entries, rather than keep a steady log of my life. It seems to me I was waiting for something to happen to me, such as the move from Pennsylvania to North Carolina. Then I would get excited enough to write about it. It's as if my diary were an old friend I would call every once in a while, just to catch up. Sometimes these gaps are weeks long. Sometimes, years.

This one is a few months after we moved to Oak Island. I am happy because I finally shook off the shadow that my sister and brother cast over me. I had a boyfriend named Jack. I had several friends. I even made the cheerleading squad. Go Cougars! I was, for once in my young life, popular. Hey, cut me some slack. I was twelve years old. I thought being popular was the most important thing in the world.

Not to mention I got my braces off, which by itself was all the reason to celebrate being alive!

We moved down to Oak Island in April so I got to spend the summer wondering what the new school year would be like. I met Tammy over that summer and we clicked. She was a few years younger than me and a couple of grades under me, but we hit it off anyways. Vicky was in my classes and also on the cheer squad with me. Tammy sort of became my out of school friend after that. Even though I didn't see her during the school day, I saw her plenty after and on the weekends. I was torn between them for a BFF. (That's Best Friend Forever to those of you unfamiliar with the term.)

It was a funny feeling to find myself the center of so much attention. I was used to folks saying, *oh, that's Ashleigh's sister,* and writing me off as if they already knew me. These kids had never met Ashleigh, and if they did, she was just my older sister. Not my predecessor. I was Jenelle Lauren Madalynn Evans. Not just *Ashleigh's sister.*

Some of you may have picked up on the fact that this is the third entry I have signed with that particular name. The quicker among you will realize that Madalynn isn't part of my name. Not then, and not now. It was a childhood fixation I had. A name I chose for myself because I liked the way it sounded. I wanted my middle name to be Madalynn, so I would sign off with it. As if that made it real. I wished everything in life was that easy. Eventually I stopped using the name, though I never forgot the allure of it.

As for Jack, there I go again with giving my heart away. Jack was the world to me at the time, though looking back I can see it was just puppy love. How silly was I? I seriously thought we would get married someday. It was hard not to think that considering he was my first, real kiss.

We were at the movies and had already been holding hands and hugging. During the film, he made his move and kissed me. It was long and sloppy and awkward. Too much teeth and lips and tongue. Maybe all first kisses are like that. Too much, too soon. At the time, I remember thinking it wasn't what I thought a kiss was supposed to be like. I was hung up on this idea it would be all fireworks and angels singing. It wasn't. Jack did his best, but to be honest, I didn't like it.

To be fair to him, he didn't get handsy or anything. It was a respectful kiss. He didn't go in for a grope or give me a hickey or anything like that. We kissed two or three more times during the movie, and they did get better with practice. I have kissed a lot since then, with more guys than I care to admit, and I will always judge each and every one of those kisses against my first one with Jack. It wasn't magical like in the movies, but it was mine. It is a memory I treasure, and one I don't mind sharing with you.

I still must've been talking to David online at the time I was 'seeing' Jack. I disappointed myself by telling him I would still date him when I was also dating Jack. I thought I was in love with both of them. My infatuation wouldn't last more than a few weeks with either of them, and I would move on to another boy. In truth, it would be a few more years before my first serious relationship. Boy crazy doesn't begin to describe me back in those days.

The last couple of lines are funny not just because of the misspelling of camera, or the way I wrote *jumping off of his jump*, or the spelling of awesome. (Grammar isn't the most important thing to a twelve-year-old girl.) The funny part is the way it shows how tomboyish I remained. There I was worried about telling two different guys that I was dating them, and in the next sentence I riding bikes off a ramp with a third guy friend.

To this day my tomboy nature is strong. If I had to choose, I'd still rather ride bikes off a ramp instead of playing house with dolls. My inner child loves stuffed animals and collecting stickers, but at the same time she wants to catch frogs and get dirty playing outside. Granted these days I have traded sneakers for dress shoes and backpacks for purses. Still, there is part of me that misses those good old days of hanging out with the guys, as one of the guys.

✳ This is the day I found my old dairy!

August 24th, 2005
10:35 p.m.

Last Day
of
Suma!

Cannot
wait
to
see
everyone!

Bye
Bye

This last entry in the Kitten Diary is from nearly a year later, and explains why this one is so short. I lost the darned thing! I don't remember if I hid it too well or misplaced it or left it somewhere and forgot about it. I started another diary in November of 2004, picking up a month from where this one left off. Through the course of the next diary, I found this one again, and documented the occasion. A lot happened between the last entry and this short but sweet declaration.

But that is in a whole other *doll* of a book altogether.

The Doll Diary

The next diary I started to journal my short life featured a popular brand of dolls on the cover. It is about the same heft as the Kitten Diary, but has more than three times the entries. I seemed to have discovered the joys of colored ink as well. The first entry is in rich mauve ink. The second in a bright red. I jump around in the colors I use for the rest of the entries, but tend to favor black. I am left to wonder if it was a mood thing or just what I had on hand. Only one entry is in pencil. Maybe that says something about me in a small way? I am willing to lay my random thoughts down in pen, where they can never be erased.

Or maybe I am reading too much into it, and I just like the way pens wrote as opposed to pencils. I am trying not to read too much into these entries as a whole, but it's hard when you have your entire life to compare and contrast. Some of these entries are about boys, some about friends, and some are about things I never thought I would do and am surprised to find I wrote about. The diary runs from November of 2004 to January of 2008. A little over three years of my young life, from the last few months of age twelve to the ripe age of sixteen.

So much happened in those three years. As we get older and we look back on our life, we see our experience in time spans. That was my youth. Those were my teenage years. That was when I was a young adult. These are my early twenties. Someday I will say that was my late thirties. Early forties. Mid-fifties. We catalog time in blocks of five, ten, even twenty years of experience.

What we don't give our younger selves credit for is the amount of experience we squeezed into even a single day. Thank goodness for diaries. I don't think I would've remembered even a quarter of the things that happened in those three years if I hadn't written them down. Again, the entries are spaced out, with days, weeks, sometimes months, between entries. As you read the inner thoughts of my younger self, you must keep in mind that I wrote in shorthand, much like my other friends. I will do my best to translate this as I go for those of you not familiar with twelve-year-old diary-speak.

Heyy!

Today I found out that I really should go back out with this really hot guy named Jack! But anyways, tomorrow I'm going to Medevil Times! In Mytle Beach! But that's after church! Ugh! At least it's only an hour. Thank God! LOL! Me and Tammy had the most funnest time today! She came with me to Whlimigton to Best Buy and I had 1500 and we spent it on candy and a viedo game! I miss Mary! I'm crying because I miss her so much! And I hate how everyone just won't stop leaving me alone! Debbie gotta stop her big fucking ▬ asshole of mouth up! I'm about to beat her up! I sware! Anyways if you flip through these pages you will see, songs, poems and other stuff! Well TTYL!

Love,
Penelle

No date on this one either, but from the hints of the entry I can place it about November of 2004. Here you can see where I thought I lost my Kitten Diary, because I speak of Jack as if it's the first time I have written about him. From August to November we were already on-again, off-again as far as seeing each other. I was in the on-again mood this time, apparently.

I was super excited about going to Medieval Times, for good reason. That place is fun! Looks like I had to wait until after church before I could go, which I give a hardy *ugh* about. That's about par for most kids in the South. Church was boring because it was stuffy and preachy and dull. No one wants to hang out in a place where they tell you everything you like to do is wrong and all of the boring stuff is all you should do. I never was much for organized religion anyways, though I attended my fair share of youth groups and bible studies. I have a very personalized idea of faith that church never quite touched. I find God in everything I see and the people I meet. I see God in my kids, in my family, and in our love for one another. Not in a building.

Tammy and I were still hanging strong. She was a great friend, even though we didn't see each other at school. It was nice to have someone in the neighborhood I could visit and do things with. But, as you can see, I missed my old friend Mary. I said in the last diary that I would only miss Lisa one hundred percent. There is no mention of Lisa here. Only Mary. Turns out she was my best friend back in Pennsylvania, and I was starting to feel the void of her absence.

Debbie was a girl at my school with a tendency to run her mouth. She was always on the edge of gossip, and in this particular instance she had been spreading some fake rumor about me. I don't remember what it was, that's how unimportant it really was. I just knew she needed to shut her fucking mouth.

Oh my, will you look at that potty mouth? Yeah, I started cussing at a young age and haven't quite stopped. You got a fucking problem with that?

You will notice I didn't include images of the promised poems or lyrics. Most of them are just hand copied works of other folks that I related too. I found some on the internet and got some from songs I liked. At this point I can't be sure what is mine and what isn't, so I just left them all out.

12/30/04

Hey! Today I went shopping at the mall! I got a sweater, Ug boots, a leather hat, and Pink Designer pants! Well anyways I'm over Matt and Jack finally and now I'm to Don! Man tonight he came over and we held hands when me & Ashleigh were walking him home. And I hate Tammy and now I found my true BFFE! Her name is Stacey Conner! She is in NJ visiting her other BFFE named Tricia. Well now if you look on the other pages it me and SC's poems and fav songs! Well I'm going because I going to sleep with the dog Don loves! Well TTYL!

♡,

Nell
(aka Jenelle)

READ BETWEEN THE LINES

Wow. So much can happen in one month. First, I just turned thirteen, so I was officially a teenager. I go from wanting to marry Jack to being over both him and some guy named Matt? And I have given up my BFF Tammy for some other new girl? Phew. That was fast!

I guess I should explain who Matt was first. He was a cute boy that lived a couple of doors down from me. We never officially dated. We just went out a couple of times and hung out with our other friends. I was kind of interested in him because my interest in Jack was waning. I think this is the first documented instance of my short attention span when it comes to guys. I clearly enjoyed the chase more than the relationship. Once I got a guy, I got easily bored and wanted a new one. This is a trend I followed until I learned that relationships are more valuable than the thrill of new love. But that won't be for a while yet.

The new boy in my life was Don. He was cool and cute, of course. We liked the same songs and bands and other stuff you think is so important at that age. He gave me this cute little stuffed dog, which I treasured and took to bed with me each night. Our time together didn't last long. By the next entry in March, he is already in the rearview mirror. I didn't know it at the time, but it was the result of a similar event in this entry that ended our relationship. I need to tell you about Stacey first, and my breakup with my old BFF Tammy.

As the school year dragged on, I saw less and less of Tammy and was starting to do more with the girls in my class. I was a cheerleader, so that ate up a lot of my time. In this span, Tammy and I had a fight over something stupid and we stopped talking to each other. In some ways, I felt like I was moving on. I was thirteen now and Tammy was only eleven. She was a kid. I was a teenager. I needed a new best friend. I found one in Stacey. She and I ruled the roost for a couple of months, which translates to forever in kid time. I used to call her SC because of her last name.

During this diary entry, Stacey was in New Jersey visiting her old friends. This left me in the company of my sister, of all people. Actually being cool for once, she agreed to help me walk my new boyfriend, Don, home. We traveled beside the waterways that run all over the islands on the coast. Don and I held hands and I was totally in love with him. He was, as I will say over and over about a number of boys, my heart.

We would repeat this journey many times over; Don coming to our neighborhood on foot, and I walking him home with anyone who would go with me so I didn't walk back alone. One night, a few weeks later, Stacey and I were walking Don home when he did a strange thing. He leaned over to Stacey, away from me, and whispered something in her ear. Which was weird, because I was on the other side of him, and apparently, the message was meant for me.

Stacey cut around the two of us, walked next to me, and whispered to me, "He wants to know if you want to have sex with him."

Okay, that was weird. Why didn't he just ask me? I looked over and he was grinning in the moonlight, his teeth and eyes glowing with a mischievous sheen. I shook my head at him, unsure what to say.

His grin faded, but he raised his eyebrows at me, as if saying, you sure?

I turned back to Stacey and whispered, "No. I am not ready. I'm not comfortable with it."

She nodded, then returned to the opposite side of him. Stacey whispered my message and it had a clear effect on Don. He looked at his feet and didn't say much else on the way home. His grip on my hand slipped away. I had disappointed him by turning down his offer.

I didn't regret it, as no girl or woman should regret such a choice. I wasn't ready and if he thought pouting about it would change that, he was wrong. We broke up shortly after that. I didn't need someone in my life that would pressure me for sex. When I was ready for it, I would choose who I wanted and when. What I didn't know then was when I was finally ready for sex, I would become obsessed with it.

One more thing about this entry, you will notice I signed it off as Nelle. Madalynn is still hanging out in the pages of the Doll Diary, but Nelle surfaces a few times too. Nelle has been a lifelong nickname for me, or rather I should say a lifelong curse. I suppose it's the natural breakdown of Jenelle. It was also something I really hated when I lived in Pennsylvania. Folks tried to call me Nelle all of the time and I avoided it like the name had the cooties. But like all things, this changed when I moved to North Carolina. On Oak Island, I liked Nelle. It made me feel like a different person. A new person. Someone I had never been before. So when it stuck this time, I let it stick, good and hard.

There is another page to this entry but I didn't include it in the scan. The upper half is another list of songs my current friends and I like. The bottom half, however, is a large announcement in those goofy, kiddy block letters we all used to draw. It proclaims in bright red ink:

Guess What?
I HATE TAMMY'S GDA!.

In parenthesis, I have added a few notes that GDA means God Damn Ass. I also underlined these notes. I must've really been mad at her for something that I can't begin to guess at now. The interesting part of all of this is that sometime later, probably only a few meager weeks, I have gone back over it in black ink. I scratched out the name TAMMY'S and wrote the initials SC. Stacey Conner. The same new BFF I couldn't get enough of.

The question is, what happened?

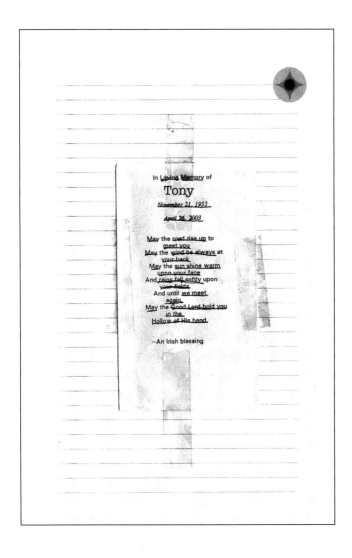

In Loving Memory of

Tony

November 21, 1955

April 26, 2003

May the road rise up to
meet you
May the wind be always at
your back
May the sun shine warm
upon your face
And rains fall softly upon
your fields
And until we meet
again,
May the Good Lord hold you
in the
Hollow of His hand.

--An Irish blessing

This isn't so much a diary entry as a keepsake. It is a small piece of paper with a poem on it. You will notice the date is older, placing this bit of memorabilia about a year before the entries it lays between. The paper is from a funeral service for my Uncle Tony. He was my mother's brother, and one of a set of twins. Uncle Tony lived his whole life with his mother, my grandmother. He couldn't really take care of himself because he had some mental difficulties. When he passed away, I kept the poem from the funeral because I thought it was pretty.

I included it here because it reminds me of a creepy story about Uncle Tony.

Before he passed away, my mother used to take us regularly to see him and my grandmother in Rhode Island. On one visit, Mom left us alone with Uncle Tony while she took our grandmother to run some errands. While she was gone, for some reason Uncle Tony began to talk to us about death and dying. As kids, we were all naturally curious and began to ask questions about the process of death. He began to go into great detail about the mortuary arts, and how organs are removed. He even talked a bit about the ancient Egyptian methods of removing your brain through your nose!

When our mother returned and asked what we did, we told her. She freaked out about it. She insisted that everything Tony told us was a lie and not to believe anything he ever says. I think she was just weirded out by the discussion.

I don't think I would like for anyone to talk about stuff like that with my kids. I would like to handle that one myself.

What I did notice from then on where the similarities between Uncle Tony and my brother Colin. I began to make connections between their habits and speech. It didn't take long for me to piece together that whatever problems Uncle Tony suffered from, Colin also suffered. It was eye opening to see your brother's possible future in such detail. Would he also end up living his whole life under Mom's care instead of having a life of his own?

I worried for him then, and I still worry for him today.

3/29 or 30/05

Heyy? Wat*z up? nmhjc ♥
Stacey got espelled from school
a long long long time ago and
ever sinced then shes acting
like a bitch? I'm not the only
one who thinks so... EVERYONE
Does? And today online we had
a fight AGAIN 4 the 2nd
time THIS WEEK? And then
we didn't finish the fight cuzz
Ashleigh started a fight w/
me and she hit me and smacked me and Punched me?
But I grabbed her ban-danna
and whipped it off then
stretched her shirt then
smacked, punch, and kicked
her? ☺? Heyy she deserved
it bad? Then I took her
bandanna and went all the
way across the street and
through it in the neighbor's
bushes? Then took her bracele
t and the~~och~~ it I.D.K.
where but I did ~~----~~
throw it sumwhere? LOLD

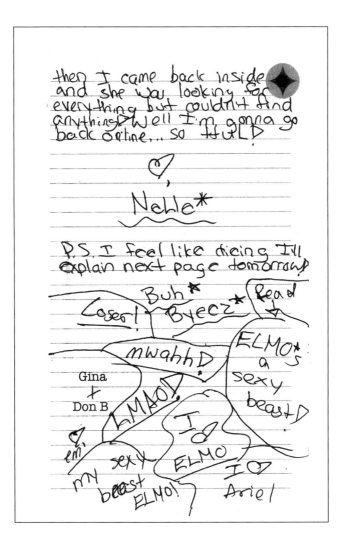

then I came back inside
and she was looking for
everything but couldn't find
anything✖ Well I'm gonna go
back online... so ttul▷

♡
'
Nehle*

P.S. I feel like dieing I'll
explain next page tomorrow

Loser! Buh* Byecz* Read

mwahh▷

ELMO*
a
s
sexy
beast▷

Gina
+
Don B

LMAO!

I ♡

♡
em?
my sexy
beast ELMO!
ELMO
I ♡
Ariel

continued....

lol

didn't
feel
like
continuing
LMAO!

Three months pass and I have already lost my new BFF. Things move fast in the world of a thirteen-year-old girl. I don't mention Tammy here, so we must've not been talking yet. I was between friends, which was a very hard state for me to be in. By now I had learned to measure my value through my contact with others. When I didn't have someone to focus on who liked me, boyfriend or BFF, I felt worthless. When I was surrounded by folks who I thought loved me, it gave me an indescribable high. I lived to be needed, and I grew needy as a result.

That neediness would be my downfall later on.

But, back to the diary. What was I up to this fine day? NMHJC! This was an abbreviation for Nothing Much Here Just Chillin'. (And if I have to explain chillin' to you, this might not be the right book for you!) It was a product of my generation to write the same way we chatted online. I suppose every generation since the invention of the internet has their own special way of talking online. I still write LOL by hand when I write notes or letters.

By this entry I was sad because Stacey wasn't going to my school anymore. She had gotten suspended from South Brunswick Middle School for violating the school's zero tolerance policy. She ended up having to go to the much-dreaded Brunswick County Academy. This was a shock to all of us, because BCA was the school for certain kinds of kids. All of the students at BCA had troubled pasts or worse, criminal backgrounds. Our parents would threaten us with the school, which was enough to snap most of us back into line. It was a bad place for bad kids, and none of us wanted to end up there, much less see one of our best friends end up there.

Stacey had been expelled several weeks before and had started attending BCA regularly. She turned into a bitch almost overnight. I made sure to ask around, to see if it was just me she was mad at, but no. She was snippy with everyone at our old school. It seemed she made all new friends at BCA. She was now friends with all of the bad kids and there was no going back.

Age and time has given me some perspective on this. Now I can see that she was cutting us out of her life because she had to. She went through such a dramatic shift—new school, new rules, new friends—she couldn't maintain the life she once had. Stacey couldn't live two lives. She had to cut one free. I just hated I was one of the ones she cut loose. I really liked her, and I felt abandoned when she left. I was just arguing with her about this when Ashleigh started yet another fight with me by doing the worst thing imaginable in 2005.

She picked up the phone while I was online and cut my connection mid-argument.

For those who have never heard of dialup, count your blessings. We used to have to use a physical phone line to dial into a server to access the internet. This wasn't like a regular phone call. If someone else picked up another phone connected to the same line, it dropped your connection, cold. I used to get into fussing matches with my family all of the time about this. I was just like any other teenager using the phone. Why couldn't they just let me use it?

My sister knew I was talking to Stacey online about stuff when she picked up the phone. She wanted to use it and instead of warning me so I could wrap things up with Stacey, Ashleigh just jerked open the line, and that dropped my connection. I was so mad at her! Like I said, this wasn't the first time. It would, however, be the last time, if I had any say in it.

I yelled at her, calling her names and the likes for dropping my connection. She responded by smacking me. So I punched her. This quickly turned into a fistfight, which as you can see I described in great detail. Funny how I left out the reasons for the fight but get every part of what happened during the battle. I guess I wrote what was fresh in my mind, the effect but not the cause. Who cared how it started? I got in my licks like I always did with her.

In this case, I also tore off her bandana and hid it. This would've been a huge blow to her because she loved her bandanas. I knew it would really hurt her if I took her bandana because it was such a safety net for her. I included a little smiley face because I was so proud of myself for thinking of it.

Yikes.

Here in my mid-twenties, that makes me cringe to read over again. I was kind of a little brat to my older sister, yet as my younger self wrote *she deserved it bad*. That bridge had burned a long time ago, and we weren't going to fix it. I wished my relationship with Ashleigh could be better. It will never be anything but what it is. When thirteen-year-old me draws a smiley face because I took something so precious from Ashleigh and hid it without hesitation or remorse, you know that relationship is beyond broken.

There are two more things here I am sure you're curious about. The first is the PS. I wrote that I felt like dying and would explain more on the next page tomorrow. Well, there is no explanation on the next page. Just a brief note that says:

LOL! Didn't feel like continuing!
LMAO!

Sorry to disappoint, but I don't remember this special reason I felt like dying. It obviously wasn't too important to me because I never got back to it. I suspect it had a lot to do with Stacey and the way she was ignoring me. I never would become friends with Stacey again, but she would betray me even more as we got older.

The last thing on this entry is the reference to Gina, Don B, and Elmo. Okay, so one of these names you know already. That's right, Elmo as in the red fluffy puppet from *Sesame Street*. Not some new boy I was chasing. Crazy sounding, isn't it? I know, right?

Gina was becoming one of my friends and she was dating a guy named Don at the time of this entry. To keep from confusing him with other Dons in the area, we called him Don B. (There were at least three other Dons in our school at that time.) Gina also had a cute obsession with Elmo. She loved the little fuzzy monster. We used to joke all of the time that Elmo was a sexy beast!

May 27th, 2005

heyy peebles ▷ he he ▷
I'm juss chillein hurr ▷ Well
now I finally have the right
guy that I ♡ 2 death...
_____Michael_____ ..and me +
Tammy are Best Friends
again and Stacey 's still a
bitch (aue BIE) and I don't
like _____Gina_____ and Debbie 's
juss anoyying and Samantha
came down tonight ▷ Wow..
tont's a lot ▷ ha ha ▷ I have
this really cool website called
www.xanga.com/CHeerx910 ▷
and it's cute and it's 4 piks
of iconz and gettin a new
page 4 layouts...▷ Ariel's helpin
me tho w/ everything. I passed
the EOG's and next week is
the last week of skowl and
I have to go to modeling skowl
too... now I get 2 b a model
yes !!! well I's gotts to go 2
sleep becuz modeling tamoro...
too... ttul ▷ lulas▷
                Buh Byes ♥33
♡ mwah ♡   tuttelz*
    -NeLLe*

This entire entry reads like a checklist of who I like and who I don't like. At the top of the list is a new boy, Michael. Even though I say I love him to death, it didn't last long. Puppy love never does. Within a month, we would not be speaking to each other and I would be on the prowl for a new guy again.

School is nearly out and I am back to being BFFs with Tammy. Stacey is just a memory by now, and a bad one. She is still hanging with the kids from BCA even though summer is nearly here. Gina had already slipped to my bad list and for a very good reason. She had stopped seeing Don B and started seeing my Don. The Don I had broken up with just a few months ago because I wasn't ready for sex. It didn't bother me too much, though. I lumped her in with folks I didn't like and moved on. Notice how bubbly and happy I am to be surrounded by people again, whether they liked me or not. My self-worth must have been through the freaking roof during this time.

How fast does the world change on you? You can see there is some reference to a website that isn't even operational anymore. If I remember it was a site for layouts for Myspace and sites like it. Myspace? Wow, now that will make you feel old.

The important part of this entry is the end, where I signed up for modeling classes. I somehow convinced my mother to let me take classes every Saturday during the summer. We took etiquette courses, classes on how to apply makeup, how to dress, and how to pose for photo shoots. It was one of the best summers of my life. After that, I knew for certain I wanted to be involved in the film industry in some way. Whether it was on or off camera.

If I only knew how I would become involved...

August 20th, 2005 (Sun.)

Heys! Uhm... i'm sooo mad and pissed off becuz of my mom! We had a fight yesterday and now I'm grounded till like ...my birthday! Well I was orignally grounded till Oct. but now it got extended. Soo now im chillen in my room till school starts next week on Thurs. and A LOT happened this summa like... got in trouble w/ a 18 year old. And now my mom doesn't love me any more, she wishes I drop-dead! And that hurts me sooo etc. much and now I have no one to love me. I'm just sitting here listening to mocking bird by Eminem. I want to be sent to a foster home. I want to tell my mom that I'm sorry for being born. Becuz I know I was just another accident.

→

I want to go in the TV Room and just tell her... "I'm sorry for all these fights I have caused our family. Soo I'm also sorry for ever being born." And what also makes me mad is that she thinks of me as a non-proud, non-caring, non-loveing, person and that she wants to send me away and never see me again. I WANT TO BE SENT AWAY! Far from ANY of my family. And I mean that. And she's also canceling modeling cuz she thinks I'm too ugly for it. Also she's canceling it cuz she tells me i'm a lil whore. So I'm in pain soooooo much and she thinks she's stressed! Aaa... NO! You have no fucking clue... NO clue how it feels NOT to be loved at all! For your mom to hate you and a dad that left you. You DONT KNOW!

no one knows! I'm so sick of crying at night and to be not kissed or even hugged at night. And to be told to go live with my dad if I hate her sooo much. But I don't, I love her. She's the best mom I can have. But she treats me like i'm not alive. And doesn't trust me with any-thing... I do. But then she won't let me kill myself. Cuz she'll go to jail or some-thing. Since she took everything out of my room ecept my karoke machine... I'll put my pain in words. And cry every night wishing I was loved. Soo this is bye untill tomoro! Bye.

Sincerely,

Jenelle
Evans

I'm talking to

Wesley

ew...

Another jump in time. This is a long and sad entry for me. It is also one I do not remember writing most of. I want to make it clear that I never made an attempt on my life when I was a kid. I sure did mention it more than once, but in reality, I never did it. I think it was all just a cry for attention. A shout into the empty universe that I just wanted to be loved.

You can see how I don't take to my journal until I have something to report. This meant I had a good summer at modeling school and the rest of the time I enjoyed playing with my friends. Life was sweet, so there was no pain to put on the paper. Until the end of August, just before school started.

It all started when I got caught hanging out with an eighteen-year-old boy. I don't even remember his name. All I remember is he was older and therefore cooler than I was. At thirteen, getting the attention of an eighteen-year-old boy was a rock star move! And please don't think too bad of the kid. We didn't kiss or anything like that. We just hung out and talked.

Well, what I didn't know was he was wanted by the police for questioning in connection with some recent robberies. The younger ones of us were already out past curfew, and here we were hanging with a wanted eighteen-year-old. Needless to say, when the cops found us, as they always did, they arrested him and marched me right on home to face my mother's wrath.

She went ballistic over this one. Not only was I out late, with a far older guy, but he was in trouble with the law? That was too much for her. I had finally pushed her across that thin line between her usual fussy self and outright anger. She screamed and yelled at me about my future and my safety, and I drowned her out with some screaming of my own. About how she was a horrible mother and didn't really love me and how I wanted to move back in with my dad. She grounded me until October, and I argued with her so much she extended it until December. Way to go, Jenelle!

To make it worse, she not only grounded me from going outside or going anywhere with my friends, she emptied my room of almost everything I owned. She took all of my electronics, my laptop, my television, everything. Anything I could entertain myself with, she took. All she left were my school books, some pens, and my diary. (And oddly enough my karaoke machine, but who would I sing to if I was grounded for the rest of my life?) I took to my diary like a convicted man about to face the electric chair and placed the blame on her.

I blamed my mom for things I am now certain she never said. I know it reads like a kid just regurgitating what she heard, but I know my mom didn't say those things to me. I must've been really upset, and made up a bunch of stuff to make myself feel better about being punished for something that, at heart, I knew was my fault. I blamed her for my stupidity. I loved my mom then and I love her now. I know we don't have the perfect relationship, but I also know she would never say that she hated me. Especially not when I was just a kid.

I did want to be sent away, but that was just a reaction to getting grounded so hard for so long. I didn't really want to tell my mother I was sorry for being born. I was a handful growing up. I know that now. My mom did the best she could with me, and I love her for it. Even if she did call me a little whore.

Yeah. That part is true. She used to throw that word around quite liberally. I guess we all have a breaking point, and hanging out with an eighteen-year-old did it for her. I was a little whore to her, and that was that. It's also true that she canceled my modeling classes, though I think my getting in trouble was just an excuse for something she was going to do anyways.

The modeling classes were starting to cost more and more, and my mother had already made noise about not being able to afford it. Once the basic classes were done, the company offered bigger and better photo packages designed to build a professional portfolio. Mom drew a line in the sand after the basic courses and we argued about it for days. As soon as I was brought home by the cops, she saw a chance to get her way, and used that as an excuse to cut me from the modeling courses.

Notice that I don't mention anyone else in this entry? No Gina, or Stacey, or even Tammy. Again, my worth is diminished because I am alone. I am worthless. I am unloved. But more importantly, I am incapable of being loved because I am worthless and alone. See the cycle? It took years of beating myself up and a few really abusive relationships to finally break out of this way of thinking. I hope my kids never feel like that. I will try to help them understand they are valuable just as they are. They are loved just as they are. They are beautiful just as they are.

My mother tried in her own way to make me understand this, but I had so much complicated stuff going on around me, I didn't listen to her. We drifted further and further apart until the gulf was too wide to even scream across. Now my son is in the middle of that gulf, separated from me by a piece of paper I foolishly signed when my back was against the wall and I felt trapped and alone.

And unloved.

This diary entry written at thirteen says so much about me and my life then and now. It is lonely. It is sad. It is rejected. I did cry myself to sleep some nights out of fear and negativity. I would like to say I will never cry myself to sleep again, but I know this isn't true. No matter how much I accomplish, a secret part of me will always be this scared thirteen-year-old girl. I will always feel awkward and maladjusted. I may smile at the camera, but sometimes I am dying on the inside. Not always, and not nearly as often as years ago, but the doubt and insecurity are still there.

It's there, somewhere, hidden under years of smiles, the assurance that everything is okay.

Heys! August 24th, 2005
Tonight is my last night
of suma vacation! Cuz I
gots shcwl tomorrow! I can't
wait! Well me & Gina r friends
again and i'm not going to
fight with her anymore. Cuz I
start all the fights.!!. LoL!
Well I found out Laura is
in my class! :) ! But Lee is
too! Ahhh! Oh well...i'll live.
Ha Ha I found my other
dairy tonight! Soo... and also
I want to go out with Wesley
soooo....etc. bad! But he
wants to see me...But I'M
GROUNDED! I'll get there
eventually... LoL! I'm soo excited I can't sleep! XD! But I'll
sleep...hopefully soon, yeahh...
Well i'ma gona go now!

Buh Byes!

Luhv.

Jenelle
Evans♡

Four days after the big blow up and everything is somehow better. Kids have that over adults. They heal quickly. Whether it's a scraped knee or a bruised ego, they recover in record time. These days when I have a blowout with my mother it takes me a week or more to get over it. Here it is four days later and I am all about the end of summa vacation! LOL!

Oh, and I found my old diary. This harkens back to the last entry in the Kitten Diary. The huge page that said this is the day I found my diary. Everything is a circle. Isn't it? Everything comes back around again, and again, and again.

Again, my focus here is on my friends and how they make me feel. I am driven by this need to impress and maintain. I make an odd confession here that I will repeat later in the last diary when I reflect on a list of my personal problems. Gina and I were friends again and wouldn't fight any more because, lo and behold, I start all the fights. I start all the fights. What a strange thing for a kid to say.

I am also interested in a new kid named Wesley. How many does that make now? I am still a virgin at this point, though I was really into kissing and holding hands. Wesley was a cute and short chapter in my life. I don't remember if we ever dated officially or if we just went out a few times. Being grounded until doomsday didn't help things.

No wonder I was so excited about school starting! At least I would get out of the house for a little while each day. Soon, none of that would matter anyways. Grounded or not, I was going to get out of the house one way or the other.

hey↓   Jan 3▓▓▓, 2006

what's up?↓ OMGAHH youh
won't BELiEVE WHAT HAPPENED
on NEW YEARS↓ hahα...
i° got fucked up↓ i smoked
pot with Torì, Diane + her
cuzin William ↓ it was funnnn!
but n✶e ways about Torì's
cousin... William, I'm rely gettin
g to know him more + more
and he is getting attached
to me↓ lol↓ he wouldn't let
me go to sleep all NiGHt↓
it was soo funn though cuz
we flirted with each other
constantly↓ i can't WAit to
see him again↓ Well i g2g↓

xoxo youh,

madalynn jenelle-lauren evans

I had just turned fourteen and this is where things start getting really interesting. Out of my entire life, this is one of those nights I can still remember vividly. I close my eyes and I go back to that night, with my friends, when I didn't have a care in the world. We were young and the future was ours. Before babies or cameras or arrests or therapy. This was our time. This was a night to remember.

I made a couple of new friends that night. The first was my new bestie Tori. I met her through Diane, who rode the bus with me. Tori and I had that instant connection that made for the best of friends. We clicked right away and discovered as the night went on that we had so much in common. She would become a life-long friend of mine, seeing me through so much and providing a shoulder to cry on more than a few times.

We are still really good friends. Even though we are grown and have our own lives, I check in with her on occasion to see how she is doing. I don't find myself doing that with many other people from my past. Tori was and is a special friend. I am blessed to have her in my life.

That's also the night I met William for the first time. This was the boy who would change my life forever. All of the other guys before him were just puppy love infatuations compared to William. He was my first, true love. I know, I know! I wrote that a half million times in my diaries and

I am sure I thought as much about each and every boy before William, but he really was different.

William was a sixteen-year-old and from a town called Gastonia, which was several hours away from Oak Island. He was down on the coast visiting his family, namely Tori because she was his cousin. He only stayed over New Year's weekend, and then had to go back to Gastonia. After that, we kept in touch by phone and online. Somewhere in there we became an item, officially dating.

To my delight, he moved back to Oak Island permanently with his family a couple of weeks later. The first trip was part of a housing search for his parents, which ended with them moving back down for good. I was thrilled, as was Tori. She and William got along so well. The three of us thought we were unstoppable. Those were good times.

As you can read, that night I started a habit that would haunt me for the rest of my life. Yeah, I am not ashamed to say I tried pot for the first time. And the second time. And the third time. When I say we stayed up all night talking, it was mostly spent smoking. I have to say, I know it's supposed to be such a horrible thing but I didn't see what the big deal was about. I felt relaxed and happy. I liked it.

I mean, think about it. My father was a notoriously mean drunk. He beat up my mom and did questionable things with my siblings whenever he started drinking. It ruined his marriage and pretty much his life. I have been in relationships where my partner turned from sweet to psycho in just a few drinks. I have seen people time and time again become monsters after consuming alcohol. In contrast, I have never been around anyone who turned mean when they smoked. Why it is so vilified when drinking is made out to be sexy?

Please don't mistake my words. For God's sake, I am not saying a fourteen-year-old should smoke. No, a four-teen-year-old should not have been smoking pot. I did. But I shouldn't have done it. No way. Still, it didn't change the fact that I did, and then I wrote about it.

Tori and William had both smoked before. When they asked if I had done pot before, I tried to play it off cool. Of course, I have, I told them. Who didn't smoke? I smoked. Everyone smoked. Don't be stupid. I am cool. I smoke.

Then I smoked my first joint. Wow. I remember feeling really silly and light in both spirit and mind. I giggled a lot. Which is saying something for a fourteen-year-old girl. Giggling is like a second language for us! I kept telling them my legs felt like Jell-O. I couldn't stand upright without slowly melting back to the floor.

I wrote about how I got fucked up and how it was so much fun. I would love to say this was the folly of youth and drugs are bad and other grown up clichés, but the truth is I really did have a good time. Yeah, I shouldn't have been smoking pot that young, but the fact remains that this was one of the best nights of my life. We didn't hurt anyone or anything. We just sat around talking and flirting and getting high. I will always remember it fondly, no matter what others think of me.

hello ↓ Feb. 13, 2006

OMG! me + William are hooked on each other we love each other sooo much i would not be alive today if it wasn't 4 him. Yeah... but he MOVED DOWN HERE! AHHH!!! But i'm fuckin grounded till Feb. 24th, 2006! Cuz me, Tori, + Ash stole from a store → Sooo yeah... but i still love Tori! ha ha! She is my BESTEST friend! But i cut myself last night cuz i got mad @ myself + my mom! William is mad and sad that i did that. But... i ♥ him sooo bad... seriously but i got to go now. Soo ♥ youh!

Tori
&
William

Jenelle

Here we are almost exactly two years from the first entry in the Kitten Diary. So much has changed. I've moved to a whole new place, made a completely new set of friends, and pissed off my mother in new and creative ways. I even started smoking pot and fell in love for real. That threshold from preteen to teenager was far behind me and I was well on my way to being a little hellion.

This is a month after the New Year's entry and I am still all about William. I will be for some time, even after we break up. But that is not for a little while at least. Here I am in love and alive because of him. I lived for William during this time. I wanted nothing more than to be with him twenty-four-seven. This was hard when he lived in Gastonia and we had to talk via the phone or the internet. Then he finally moved down and we got to hang out as much as possible. *As much as possible* wasn't very often at the time I wrote this entry because I was, surprise-surprise, grounded yet again. This time, though, it was with fairly good reason.

I got caught shoplifting.

Actually, it wasn't just me. Tori and Ashleigh and I all got busted for stealing a variety of stuff from a department store. Makeup and sunglasses and other stuff I am sure we could have afforded. It wasn't about the money though, was it? It was about the thrill. It was about seeing what we could get away with. Or, in this case, what we could get caught trying to get away with.

Most department stores employed a security team to watch for shoplifters. They had cameras all over the place, and not to mention the employees were watching us as well. I am sure we made quite the sight; a trio of giggling girls stuffing our pockets while keeping a casual lookout for each other. I remember that I didn't care if I got caught or not. I think I wanted to get busted. I wanted to see what kind of reaction that would provoke in our mom.

I know it might be surprising to read that Ashleigh was involved in our little criminal jaunt. I think she was just bored and came with us because she didn't have anything else to do that night. Our mother was a school bus driver at the time, so she was home most nights since she worked in the day. Funny thing is, she would start working for the same department store a couple of years after this incident.

We got busted by the local security and ushered into custody in his office to wait for an officer of the law to collect us. While we waited, the security guard questioned us for his own paperwork. First, he gave us the usual speech about how much trouble we were in, and how he would have to call our moms and report what we had done.

Ashleigh started to get nervous about that. She began to fidget and sweat. I wasn't worried about it. I had been in trouble so much, it didn't bother me. Ashleigh wasn't as adventurous as I was. In other words, she didn't get in as much trouble as I had, even though she was much older than me. Speaking of age, that was the security guard's first question.

"How old are you?" he asked me.

"Fourteen," I said.

He made a note of it, then turned to Tori. "How old are you?"

"Thirteen," she said.

The guard made note of that, then turned to Ashleigh. "And how old are you?"

Ashleigh was visibly sweating by then. I could tell she was gonna freak out any moment. I was torn between telling her to suck it up and trying to help her calm down. I opted to keep my mouth shut, because the security guy didn't look like he was in the mood for family drama.

"How old are you, missy?" he asked Ashleigh.

She hesitated, letting out a little groan.

"Well?" the guard said.

Ashleigh bit her lip, then said, "If I say I am sixteen, will you still call my mom?"

The security guy smiled at her. "Look, kid, if you're sixteen, we won't have to call your mother."

My sister let out a sigh of relief and relaxed. "Well in that case, I am sixteen."

"Good," he said. "And in that case, you can go to jail." He stood and pointed at Tori and me, adding, "You two can wait here for your mothers to come and get you."

Ashleigh went white at those words. Her lip began to tremble and I could see she was doing everything she could not to start crying.

"No!" she shouted. "I'm fifteen! I'm fifteen!"

The guard rolled his eyes and wrote something on his pad. He didn't have any other questions for us. We sat there in silence for a good twenty minutes, staring at each other and the security guard behind the desk. Finally, the officer arrived and the security guard explained the situation.

He pointed to me first. "That one is fourteen."

He shifted his finger to Tori. "That one is thirteen."

He pointed to Ashleigh last, saying, "And that one doesn't know how old she is!"

Tori and I laughed at that. I don't think we got in trouble for laughing, because even the officer was laughing about it. Ashleigh was the only one not laughing about it. In the end, our mother didn't punish us too badly, because we were only grounded until February 24. It was already February 13. I could do that short of a stint standing on my head!

The other half of the entry deals with a more serious topic. I tried cutting myself for the first and last time. It wasn't anything serious, just a few scratches on one arm. I tried it out because I had heard other kids at school talk about how it relieved stress and helped them get over bad stuff that was happening around them.

As I said earlier, I only cut myself the one time. I didn't make a habit of it nor did I want to do it on a regular basis. I don't know why the other kids talked it up, but in my experience it did nothing but cause me more pain, and leave behind marks I couldn't easily explain. Marks both Tori and William were mad about.

I tried to hide it from them, but they found out and got so upset with me. William made me promise I wouldn't hurt myself again. I agreed, but not just for him. I was done with that kind of attention seeking. It wasn't worth the trouble. It seems I did have a limit after all.

April 19, 2006

Hey! It's like 11:45 pm
and Tori, William, and
Lucy are all meeting
each other and I want
to go but they won't let
me. They said they don't want
to even RISK me getting
in trouble again! But I
wanna go sooooo bad!
Oh well... I'll wait until
the summer... I'm guna go
experiment with some pills
though like Methylphenidate.
it's in my moms car though.
But at least tomorrow is
4/20 BUDDIE! NATIONAL
SMOKE DAY! I'm guna
get FUCKED! UP TOMORO
he he! That makes me soo
ticked though cuz they
are having fun without me!
I just gotta get over it...
they just called me. HOLD
ON!

This was a late-night entry I made because I was jealous of my friends going out when I couldn't. Surprisingly enough I wasn't grounded during this time, and my friends weren't going to let me get in trouble. Oak Island had an eleven o'clock curfew for minors. As an adult, I think that is a fantastic idea. As a kid, it sucked. We used to stay out after eleven all of the time, and had our butts escorted home by the police all of the time too.

On this occasion, my friends had all decided they were going to meet late and break curfew so they could just hang out for a bit. They had talked about it online and carefully planned the whole thing. They even told me about it, with the stipulation that I wasn't allowed to join them.

Now, on the surface this may seem cruel. As if Tori and her other friend Lucy were rubbing it in my face that they got to hang out without me. But in reality, they were looking out for me. You see, my mother thought Tori was a horrible influence on me. Yet she was always watching out for me, telling me not to do stuff that she knew would make mom angry or get me into trouble. I never listened to her. I think it was all part of my lashing out at my mother growing up. I wanted to see how mad I could make her, and I pushed it harder and harder each time.

I start this entry with good intentions. I didn't go and hang out. I stayed home like a good girl and resisted the temptation to go and hang with the gang after curfew. Then

I start to talk about drugs with a surprising casual passivity. I had only been smoking pot for a couple of months, and here I act like I had done it for years. The thing about the pills was a passing thought more than anything else. I had heard kids at school talk about their experiences with pills. Eventually I did experiment with pills, but that is yet another entry we will talk about later.

This diary entry ends abruptly with a dramatic flick of ink. I didn't even get back around to signing it. My friends had called me to see how I was holding up without them and that was all I could take. I decided to sneak out anyways and meet up with them, whether they wanted me there or not. I tricked Tori into telling me where they were, got my stuff together, slipped out of the window, and was off to join them.

I met up with my friends sometime after midnight and although they were mad at me at first for putting myself at risk, we had a great time. We hung out and talked and just enjoyed ourselves. About two in the morning I decided I needed to go home. The gang walked me back to my house and I said goodnight to each of them, giving William a nice warm kiss before slipping into my room through the open window once more. I left the lights off so I wouldn't wake anyone else in the house. I was so exhausted, I kicked off my shoes and went right to bed. Or at least I tried to go to bed.

To my surprise, my mother was sleeping in my bed! She woke up when I tried to climb onto the mattress beside her. A screaming match ensued and once again I found myself grounded. It was worth it though. That was another night I will always remember.

I don't reference it in my entry, but by this time I had started doing something else that later on would cause me even more trouble than smoking pot. I started having sex. I may have been a bit boy crazy before this, and I certainly gave my heart away to each of them far too quickly. I hugged and kissed and necked and generally made out with some of them. Yet I never went *all the way* with a boy until William.

I used to sneak out of the house and sneak into William's room and spend the night without either of our parents knowing about it. After a couple of months of dating, and sleeping in the same bed a few times a week, I finally decided I was ready. I asked him one night if he wanted to have sex. In all of that time, William never tried to force himself on me. We would hug and kiss, and the petting would get pretty heavy, but that was about it.

The night I offered my virginity to him, William made double sure I was ready. He didn't jump me right away and take it. He asked if it was what I really wanted. I told him it was. He explained that he would take his time and make it good for me. He had a regular partner once before and knew what he was doing.

And he did. William was gentle and sweet and slow. He didn't just have sex with me. He made love to me. It hurt like hell, and I bled, both things he apologized for even though neither things were his fault. All in all, it was a good first time. Better than a lot of stories I hear from my girlfriends. I had a guy who took the time needed to make it special for me. I will always love him for that.

We started having sex pretty regularly after that. William was a good first lover and I got over the pain and started enjoying myself. He taught me a lot. Despite how good it was, we would only last a few more weeks thanks to my crazy nature.

April 29, 2006 Saturday
11:15 p.m.

Hello! I'm grounded again! this time because i skipped school AND ranaway from my house. I'm only grounded till June.. lol... well i C7William SOOOOOOO BAD! And he is muh fuckin world right now holding me together. DAMN ZOE BARKED AND IT SCARED ME! rre ways... i'm just sitting here chillen... i feel bad though because i lie too much to everyone i mean not to my friends though everyone but them (Zoe is bout 2 bark again.) man i cannot believe i was about 2 kill myself and film it. i'm scared cuz Tori told William something + now he is mad @ me and i don't know what 4. well im guna go cuz i wana find out what it IS.

xoxo
Jenelle
Evans

Ten days later and grounded for something completely different again? Oh, Jenelle, will you never learn? No, I didn't. I kept running away to different friends' houses where I would spend the night. My mother would always find me and drag me back home. This grounding came from skipping school. Staying overnight at a friend's without asking was one thing. Skipping school was something else.

I am all about William in this entry as well. Little did I know he was already slipping away from me. My tendency to take everything too far and seek the extreme in all things was driving a wedge between us, and soon he would call us quits. I know how screwed up I am, because I mention how I lie to everyone. Not to my friends but everyone else. I mostly lied to my mom about everything in my life. I never had an honest conversation with her.

There is a bit there about wanting to kill myself and film it. Another cry for attention, I am certain of it. This time I got the attention I wanted when Tori told William about the plan. It upset him and he decided enough was enough. I wasn't stable enough for a relationship. He was tired of investing time in a girl who thought cutting herself or trying to kill herself were just things to try out for the fun of it.

He was done with me, but I was nowhere near done with him.

July 11, 2006

OMGAH! Since i last talked 2 you me & William brokeup then he went out with Lucy and then he and i are friends w/ benefits. And today me & Ashleigh got into a huge fight and im going to ECHS! Me & Stacey are friends + to this day I ran away 3 times! LONG STORY! But me & William are not going to go back out + I'm pissed about it. i hate my life! i feel like killing myself! William won't talk to me like hardly no more and i'm sick of all this stupid shit

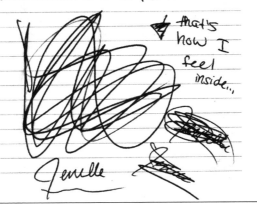

that's
how I
feel
inside...

Jenelle

Stacey is back in my life, though briefly. It was summer again, so it didn't matter what school any of us attended. Stacey was part of my neighborhood crew again, and that made me happy. Which I needed because I had enough other stuff to worry about. One was the new school year. I was going to start taking Early College High School (ECHS) classes and the stress of it was bearing down on me hard. My mother was happy about it, and I was too, but I knew if I didn't do well it would just go into the pile of things I screwed up.

I was always a smart kid. I read several levels above my class, and usually made great grades when my *extracurricular activities* didn't get in the way. The thought of early college courses delighted me because I couldn't wait to be done with high school. I wanted to move onto college and get out of my house.

I had run away a couple more times, though they were more like slipping out and sleeping over at friend's houses. When it came to running away, I never packed a bag and left home on a bus. I never hitchhiked out of town. I never went further than Tori or William's house. I just thought of it as running away. I think it was just a touch of the dramatic coming out in me.

Speaking of dramatic, William and I were officially done. Or were we?

He broke it off with me one night, saying that it was over for good. He enjoyed the time we spent together, and the sex of course, but he was starting to get tired of my drama. It seemed to him like I wanted to get into trouble all the time and stay in trouble. He was tired of apologizing to my mother for my behavior.

Tori felt the same way about it. They were worried I was on a path to self-destruction. Neither William nor she was responsible for me or my actions. I thought I knew exactly what I was doing. (spoiler alert: I didn't!) I also didn't plan on letting them escape my life quite so easily.

Even though we broke up, William kept coming back to me for the occasional hookup. I was so infatuated with him, I was all too eager to give him what he wanted. We would spend the night together, then he wouldn't talk to me for a week or so. Then he would come back again. He called this *friends with benefits*. I didn't care what he called it. I called William mine.

He dated other girls in between this, like Tori's friend Lucy. This tore me apart, seeing him with other girls when I knew he wanted to come back to me. And come back he did, time and time again. Each encounter I would work on him a little more, trying to wheedle my way back into his good graces. I would call him just to talk. I would message him online just to say hello. I would take him to my bed whenever he wanted. You know, like couples do.

We weren't a couple. We were just friends with benefits. And, thanks to my badgering, we soon lost our friendship status. After a few weeks of this slow chipping away at this wall he put between us, he finally exploded. I woke one morning to my mother tossing a letter on my bed. She said it was taped to the front door. The letter was from William.

It basically said that he didn't want anything else to do with me. That I needed to get my act together and leave him alone. I was too extreme. If I could calm the fuck down and stop pestering him for a relationship that wasn't going to happen, then maybe we could be friends again. I knew that meant he still wanted to screw around.

It was sad, and it said a lot about me and my desperation for approval, but I followed the advice in the letter. I left him alone and when he came to me for sex, I gave it to him. In my mind the occasional fuck was far better than no contact with him at all. I loved him and if this was the only way I could see him, then so be it.

This set the tone for most of the relationships in my life. Instead of getting over him and moving on, I learned to become a doormat for him. I would repeat this scenario over and over and over throughout my life, letting myself become an extension of some guy's ego and a tool for them to use. I was always looking for people to complete me because I had a void in my heart that was so empty I would fill that void with anything anyone would give me.

It took a long time to realize that the void in my heart didn't need to be filled with attention or things or sex. It needed the simplicity of love. Love from my children. Love from my fiancé. Love from my friends. And yeah, even love from my family, as screwed up as we all are. But the biggest help, the love I have had to force myself to accept, was love from myself. Forgiveness and compassion for my own destructive behavior, most of it directed at myself. I had to forgive and love me.

I had to learn to love Jenelle for Jenelle's sake. I had to become my own BFF. Yet that wouldn't happen for a long time, and after two kids, several boyfriends, and a television series.

Look at me there, fourteen years old, maintaining my self-esteem by sleeping with a guy who obviously doesn't want me. Look at the scribble at the bottom of the page. Look at the note I wrote beside of it.

That's how I feel inside.

That was exactly how I felt inside. A scribbled-up mess of crisscrossed lines. A tangle of knots that no one could undo. I couldn't even sign my own name without scratching it out. I felt like a cluster fuck that did not deserve to live.

Omgah...
i'm cryin right now
William keeps talking to Stacey on
the phone + calling her i'm not
mad @ Stacey... i'm sick of this
SHiT B/C everyth
everytime me + William hook
up for like 1 month, he
finds someone else,... i love
him so much, you don't even
know... no one does, he's my
fuckin HEART i never
'd someone as much as i
did William ... i'm serious
well i'm guna go ...
BYE
xoxo Jenelle

This entry is a mess, like I was. It's all over the place and crazy. I didn't date it but I think it is at the beginning of September, right after school started. I was at my height of my obsession with William and he was still using me for my body. To make matters worse, he had gotten himself expelled from our school at the end of last year and in the new school year he started going to the much-dreaded *bad school*. That's right, he started going to Brunswick County Academy.

And guess, just fucking guess, who he started talking to there?

Fucking Stacey! It's like the setup from some cheap, poorly written young adult romance novel. My ex-best friend and my ex-boyfriend hooking up? It killed me inside to know they were spending time on the phone together. He would still come to me for a quick screw, but talk to her on the phone. How could he not see that was wrong? How could he not see how much I loved him?

And oh man, I thought I loved him so much. I wanted him to love me as much, but that was never going to happen. I was such a fool. Such a god damned fool! I didn't even have a friend to help me out and get me through this hard time. Tori started hanging out more and more with Lucy and less with me. I wouldn't be surprised to learn I had pushed her away from me too by the way I chased danger. I had lost another best friend because I couldn't cope with things normally.

That's the thing about looking at something years later. You see it with a more experienced eye, and a boatload of understanding. I wished I could go back to my younger self and say, hang in there! This pain will go away. William isn't the end all and be all of men. You will find better and do better and be better. And I would find better fairly soon, but first I would try something on a whole new level of dangerous.

Because there was no one there to stop me, and I couldn't stop myself.

Oct. 28, 2006
29 lol...

hey! gah... i got NEWS to tell you! lmao! ever since we last talked i overdosed on pills + i go out with Neil he's now my other ♥ + we even got our kids names... lol... Jon Bonnet + Vahn Luke Jones.

Here is the shortest of any entry across the three diaries, yet it packs the biggest punch. I love how the entry is so casual about two such diverse events in my life. On the one hand, I nearly overdosed on pills and on the other I started dating a really good guy. Neither are related in any way. The pills came first, then I met Neil. I think if I had met him first, I wouldn't have taken the pills.

You might remember from several entries ago that I said I wanted to start experimenting with pills. Well, I never got around to getting into my mother's purse for her pills, but I did something else. School had just started and that meant new gossip. The new thing that all the kids were talking about was how taking a high dose of a certain kind of decongestant would make you high. (Boy, I was so easily influenced by those around me.) The kids said it gave you a weird trip that you would never forget. A weird trip sounded like fun to me. I was bored and lonely and looking for something new to do. And do I did. A lot of it.

Basically, I overdosed on decongestant.

Everyone hears the word overdose and they immediately connect dots that aren't there. I am sure some of your minds are full of images of this dramatic teenager taking a bunch of pills and leaving a note for my mother to discover after I am gone. You can see my mother finding my nearly lifeless body and calling 911 and rushing me to the emergency room. You can just picture some nurse pumping my stomach in order to save my young life. You can see the doctors standing over me, clicking their tongues and telling me how I was so close to dying and how lucky I should feel to be alive.

Right?

Wrong.

You have to keep in mind first of all that I wasn't trying to kill myself. I was trying to get high. Yes, it was in one of the most stupid ways imaginable. I won't deny that. Somehow, I managed to get ahold of a box of twenty-four decongestant pills. I don't remember if I took them from home or if I grabbed them from somewhere else. I just know I got them and decided to give it a try. I was hanging out in the park with a friend, just down the street from my house. The plan was to get high, hang out for a while, then go home and sleep it off.

I took six pills at first, then waited. I got a little lightheaded but nothing else. I talked with my friend and sat around for about two hours or so. I got nothing from it, so I took six more. I waited again. This time there was a little dizziness, but not the weird, trippy high I had heard so much about. I was disappointed, to say the least. Where were my hallucinations? Where was my unusual insight to the universe? All I got was a queasy feeling.

So, I took six more.

By now I was starting to feel the effect. I was light headed and unfocused. I thought, surely, I was on the right path. I was headed for the best trip in my life, and I couldn't wait. Another thought occurred to me just then too. By now I was several hours in and I began to worry I had spaced the pills out too much. I was concerned that the time between the first six and the last six was too long and I wouldn't get the full effect.

So, you guessed it, I took the last six.

After this dose, I sat and waited for my promised trip. What I got was dizzy and nauseous and unbalanced. I knew something wasn't right when my heart started beating really fast. I had some chest pains and felt really sick to my stomach. That's when I decided to go find my mom and tell her what I had done. Again, I didn't want to die, I just wanted to try something new.

My mother was in the kitchen when I got home, stumbling through the door. As soon as she laid eyes on me she knew something was wrong. She was screaming at me, but I could tell it was in a panic. I confessed what I had done to her between excited breaths. My mother kept yelling at me while she checked me over to make sure I was okay.

Instead of the big drama of rushing me to the emergency room, my mother had me lie down on the couch to rest. I did as she instructed, laying down and trying to let this thing pass. I know some of you are probably freaking out about this. I had just told my mother I took too many decongestant pills and she didn't rush me to the hospital.

To be fair, I don't think I let on exactly how many pills I took. I think I may have told her that I took a few, as in six or so. I certainly didn't tell her I took a whole damned box!

And in her defense, I didn't die. I lay there and rested and the whole thing passed. It took a while, sure, but I was okay in the end. She also kept a careful eye on me, checking on me periodically and making sure I wasn't showing signs of something worse than what I had already told her. And yelling at me the whole while, of course. I survived, none the worse for wear, and my mother didn't have to explain to CPS why I took a whole box of decongestant.

After my poor excuse for a trip I found something much better than a handful of pills. Neil was quite a guy. He was so very different from the usual kid I was attracted to. Neil was a good kid. And not just nice, he was super good as in well behaved and never got into trouble. He was a straight-laced Christian, with a minister for a mother and a general wholesome attitude. He was such a good influence on me. I was in love with a good guy for once.

But alas, nothing lasts forever.

Nov. 2nd, 2006...
hey whats up? im PiSS
ED off cuz my fuckin
mom... gawd damn! i'm
cryin idk why but i just
am. i'm listening to
Godsmack. Gawd i just
wana go to the beach,
listen to my iPOD, &
think. Just to think &
gather thoughts. My
thoughts are just scatt-
ered into a pile of mess
that i should clean. i'll
clean it tomorrow. i love
writing to you because
you know EVEYTHING
that goes on in my
life. Weather you under-
stand or not... you listen
& you make me happy.
i don't even know who
i'm writing this to...
but i just feel as if
it's the right thing to
do... just spill my heart
out into this dairy.
nte ways... i ♥ Neil sooo
mucho & wish i can
→

talk to him but...
my mom wont let me
talk now... ugh! see now
your calming me down.
i'm relaxed! thx! !!
but seriously i'm in
fuckin L O V E! i mean
i'll admit my 1st ♥ was
William ... but Neil ... OMG
is sooooo
mucho better! HA! !!
did i tell you i'm gettin
a Teacup Chawawa
soon? yepppperz! i can't
wait! ima name it
Chewy or Jonebonnet!
ORR Mackenzee !!!
i'm sooo BORED!
well ima go ily!

xoxo jenelle

P.S.
JENELLE + Neil = ♥

Wow. Kind of eerie, isn't it?

It's like I stopped and addressed the camera during the filming of a movie of my own life. I didn't know to whom I was writing at the time, but I took a moment to reach across the void and say thank you. It turns out I was writing it to myself, and to you, dear reader, whomever you are! Here we sit, reading this diary together as I explain things to you from my perspective ten years later. How is that for a weird trip?

I said at the beginning that my diaries were a way for me to express myself without judgment or remorse. I realize that releasing them to the public like this will probably bring a whole lot of both down on me in the long run. Still, I am glad we took this journey together. Yeah, I know there is a whole third diary to get through, but this next to last entry represents the last of my childhood innocence. I want to thank you for witnessing it with me. Like the smoke of a summer campfire, it will vanish soon enough. And when it is gone, there is no bringing it back.

I was just getting into Neil at this time, and I think that is why this entry is so much calmer and relaxed when compared to my other ones. I had finally moved on from William. He stopped calling on me for sex and I stopped putting my all into getting him back. Neil helped with that. He gave me my self-worth by not expecting anything from me more than my company.

We met in ECHS classes, and were about the same age. We went on a few dates at first, with either my mother or his mother driving us to the movies and other places. We held hands and talked about the future. He was so different from William. Although William didn't expect sex at first, once he got it, that's all he seemed to want from me. Neil bought me a Bible and taught me about the Christian faith.

I actually started going to church with him. He lived about forty minutes from me, so our parents would have to shuttle us back and forth in order for us to spend time together. I finally asked his mother if I could spend the night and to my surprise she agreed. Though Neil had to give up his bed to me while he slept on the couch. He didn't mind though. We would stay up late and talk and stuff.

I know you're thinking that stuff was sex. It wasn't. At least, not at first. Neil was a virgin when I met him, and he wasn't in any rush to change that. After a few months of dating, while I was over one night, I asked him if he wanted to have sex with me. He was shy about it, but after some discussion and thought, he decided he did want to give his virginity to me.

We made love as quietly as we could in his bed, then he slipped back downstairs to sleep it off on the couch. We became regular lovers after that, sneaking it in whenever we could. We ended up dating for a little more than a year. You will notice there is a year-long gap between this entry and the last one. I think that is because I was genuinely happy for once. I didn't have any drama to report or schemes to document. I wasn't grounded forever or mad at the world.

I was in love with a sweet guy and everything was going to be okay.

Until he broke it off one day, very suddenly. I was at home wondering what Neil was up to because he wasn't online. He called me from the movie theater, of all places. I asked him what he was doing, and he said he was calling to break up with me. He was actually at the movies with another girl. A girl he had met a few weeks ago and wanted to go out with instead. A girl he was at the movies with instead of me, his actual girlfriend!

I was crushed. My whole perfect world caved in on itself. I was loved. I loved him. What happened? I asked him exactly that and he said something I will never forget.

"I like her better."

In my adult mind, I have created the sitcom scenario where he accidentally asks this new girl out while still dating me. Instead of having the balls to tell me straight away, he decides to go out with her first to see if it works out. He has a crisis of faith in the middle of the movie, and steps out to call me and confess all. I wished it had played out differently. I wished he had called me to say he was sorry and would never do it again.

Yet no, that's not what happened. For all I know he had been playing me for weeks with this girl. I never did find out the details, though I certainly tried. There was only one way he could have gotten to the movies, much less with a date. His mother had to drive him. I called her as soon as he hung up on me, to ask her how she could drive him and another girl to the movies.

She said that Neil was her son and she would do anything to make him happy. If this new girl made him happy, she was sorry it hurt my feelings, but that was that. I wasn't getting Neil back. He was gone into the arms of another girl. I was through.

I raged and cried and fussed and freaked out. Something I didn't do, was write a diary entry about it. That kind of surprises me, as I seemed to turn to my diary in times of strife. Though in truth, I don't need a diary to remember this hurt. I was devastated. This breakup was something I would never quite bounce back from. I had just gotten over the whole doormat attitude with the trouble maker William, when a supposed good kid like Neil dumps me without warning. This sent me careening back into the arms of bad boys.

The first one was named Andrew

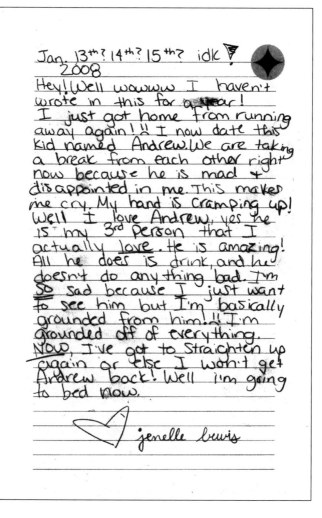

Jan. 13th? 14th? 15th? idk
2008
Hey! Well wowww I haven't
wrote in this for a year!
I just got home from running
away again!!! I now date this
kid named Andrew. We are taking
a break from each other right
now because he is mad +
disappointed in me. This makes
me cry. My hand is cramping up!
Well I love Andrew, yes he
is my 3rd person that I
actually love. He is amazing!
All he does is drink, and he
doesn't do anything bad. I'm
so sad because I just want
to see him but I'm basically
grounded from him!!! I'm
grounded off of everything.
NOW, I've got to straighten up
again or else I won't get
Andrew back! Well i'm going
to bed now.

jenelle lewis

My last entry in the Doll Diary sees me a little over a year later, and with a new man. Emphasis on man. Andrew was twenty-two when we first discovered each other. Six years older than I. Talk about trouble, he was a whole bucket load!

We met online the October before this entry, and talked through messages for a couple of weeks. Just after my birthday in December we finally met in person. By this diary entry I am already on a "break" from him because we were fighting about something stupid. I am so enamored of him that I hold up his drinking habit as a good thing. *All he does is drink?* He did drink. A lot. Ugh. I got so sick of it. I mean I like a beer every now and again (now that I am of age of course) but he stayed wasted most of the time.

At sixteen I thought that was so cool. He drank more than he should, and I thought it was so adult and fascinating. After this entry, we got back together and I fell even harder and deeper in love with him. There was no going back for me. I was hooked on Andrew and nothing could separate us. Ever.

Not even the school system. Andrew used to come and pick me up from school every day and we would go hang out until that evening, then I would go home. Well, the school system didn't like the idea of me having an older guy come and get me. They threatened to suspend me if they caught him on the school grounds again. I didn't listen and got suspended anyways. After that he used to park down the street and I would walk down from the school and get in his car and leave with him. What can I say, I was crazy about the guy.

With Andrew, I found myself in the same position I was in with William. I became a doormat for the guy. He came and got what he wanted from me, when he wanted it, and I waited for him to tell me what to do. We had to talk when he wanted to talk, no matter the odd hours. We had to go out when he wanted to go out. We did what he wanted to do. My world revolved around Andrew.

By December of 2008 my life took a sharp turn when I missed my first period. A few weeks later I suspected I was pregnant. At first I wasn't sure what to do. Who could I tell? Where could I get help? Andrew wouldn't want a baby with me, I was only seventeen! I knew my mother would kill me. It was the most frightening moment of my life. Even with another life growing inside of me, I had never felt so alone.

I told Andrew about it first. He was a little surprised but didn't get upset about it. In truth, I think he didn't care. He put on a smile to make me happy, yet in my gut I could feel that he wasn't interested in having a kid. I knew then he wouldn't stick around. And he didn't.

While I was pregnant, his family moved to Laurinburg, and he went with them. I don't know if he told them I was pregnant or not. I never talked to them about it. They never

120

showed any interest in talking to me about it or making any arrangements for their grandchild. When they moved away, I never heard from his parents again. Andrew came and went from my life too, but more on that in a bit.

As for my mother, well, that reveal was a little bit different. I didn't really tell my mother about my pregnancy. She sort of guessed. Three months in, I started having trouble hiding the obvious changes in my body. It didn't take long because she walked in on me when I was taking a bath. She must have had a glimpse of my growing baby bump, because the next day she brought me a pregnancy test and told me to take it in front of her.

The test was positive. She wasn't happy. She freaked out and started screaming at me about how my life was over and stuff like that. Still, after she calmed down, my mother showed remarkable support for my situation. I thought she would kick me out and force me to find my own way after making such a huge mistake. I thought maybe she would want me to get rid of it, by either adoption or other means. Instead, there was never any question about what to do except go forward. She basically said I had messed up, there would be consequences, and I would have to face them. I would have this baby and I would raise it and she would help me.

I didn't know she meant she would take the baby away from me.

Now that I have the advantage of looking back on everything that has happened, I wonder if my mother didn't just want another child of her own? She's always loved kids and seemed happiest when she was mothering us. I was her youngest child, who was now old enough to have kids of my own. I wonder if that left her feeling empty. I wonder if she had secretly looked forward to the birth of my child. After all, she was quick to take custody from me and has always tried to raise Jace as her own.

Either way, I was a pregnant teenager with almost no support from the father. Throughout my pregnancy, Andrew came and visited a few times. My mother would let him stay overnight, though she wasn't happy about it. She had nothing to worry about though, I wasn't interested in sex. Hell, I was already pregnant. Andrew was more interested in partying with his friends and getting drunk than spending time with his pregnant girlfriend. Not to mention he was broker than fuck and didn't have a job. What in the heck did I ever see in him? I had no idea how I was going to have a baby, much less raise one with no income.

About six months into my pregnancy, I found my answer.

Between the Pages

A few years passed between the Doll Diary and the Zebra Diary. A lot of memories were created. A lot of things happened. A lot of pain and happiness. And a lot of it was captured on camera.

So there I was, seventeen years old and six months pregnant. I didn't have any money. I didn't have much support. I didn't have a fucking clue what I was going to do. I found solace in the one place that most Americans find peace these days, in television. I was hooked on a show that I completely identified with. All of the characters spoke to me and seemed to understand me and my situation. How could they not? They were all pregnant teenagers too!

I am talking, of course, about the show *16 and Pregnant* that airs on MTV. I watched every episode with an assured comfort that I wasn't the only one who made stupid mistakes. There were other girls just like me out there. It was like having my own circle of pregnant friends. One afternoon, I watched to the end of one episode and before it finished, an announcer said the network was looking for new moms for the next season. They were having a casting call for the show. If you were a pregnant teenager, they wanted to hear from you.

Wait a minute. I was a pregnant teenager.

I went to the computer and looked up the website. The casting call was real! They were looking for all kinds of pregnant teenage girls. True, I wasn't sixteen right then, but I did get pregnant at sixteen. I followed the instructions and emailed them my information. I waited with excitement. How cool would it be to appear on MTV? And the money would help so much.

The next day I was out with my mother when MTV called on my cell phone. I was so excited I had her pull over so we could both talk to them. I quickly explained it to my mom, and she agreed to sign off on it. Within a few weeks, we had the paper work, and they began filming in June of 2009.

Signing on with the show changed my life forever. Some for better and some for worse. It was and continues to be an invasive process. Please don't misunderstand me—I'm not complaining about being on television. No one makes me do these shows, and I must admit I do enjoy the attention and, of course, the financial aspect. But a simple truth remains: it is harder than it looks. Putting your life out there to be judged by everyone around you is difficult. Emotionally. Physically. Spiritually. It drains you. It shapes you. Sometimes, it damages you.

Having a child can also do those things to you, but there is a vast difference between the two. On August 2, 2009, I gave birth to my first child, JaceVahn Evans. Much like signing onto a television series, Jace changed my life forever. In his case, it was all for the better. My son gave me a connection to the world in a way I never knew possible. He gave me a peace and satisfaction I didn't know existed. I looked into his little face for the first time and knew real love. I thought all of those guys in my life would complete me, but it turned out I only needed one little guy to fill that gap in my heart.

The beginning of the birth was a comedy of errors when it came to trying to contact his dad. The day I went into labor, I was at home on the phone with Andrew, arguing like always. He said something that pissed me off so I hung up on him. Served him right. When I stood to get on with my day, warm wetness ran down my thighs, soaking my pants.

Aw fuck, my water broke.

My first instinct was to call Andrew back and tell him to get his ass into town! But when I called him back, he wouldn't answer. That's right. I hung up on him during our argument, so he ignored my phone calls. That was the level of maturity I was dealing with from a man six years older than me. No bother, I had my mother to help. I found her, explained what was happening, and she got me to the hospital. I tried to call Andrew several times during the trip, and after six or seven tries he finally answered with that *what in the hell do you want* attitude.

I told him what in the hell I wanted.

Andrew arrived at the hospital while I was in labor. Then he left to drink with his friends. I think it was then that I realized I had to cut him out of my life. The man couldn't put down a drink long enough to watch the birth of his own child? Never mind the red flags leading up to this realization. Never mind how he treated me and my mother. I had had enough of him.

We broke up shortly after that. I was done with Andrew. I didn't need such an asshole around me and my child. He didn't put up much of an argument. Andrew went back to his parents in Laurinburg and I only saw him once after that. He never comes to see his son though he still calls and says he wants to. It just never happens. He signed away his custody and I don't know if he will ever be in his son's life again. I lost custody, too, but in a different way.

The offer to do the *Teen Mom 2* show came up and I jumped on it with glee. The money from the first one was such a blessing, and I thought I was getting used to living my life on camera for a few weeks a year. I soon found myself super stressed and worn down. I had just had a baby, sent the father away, and was filming a new series. Raising Jace was proving to be more difficult than I expected. Being a mom was hard work! I was tired and needed a break from it all. One night, my mother convinced me to go out with my friends so I could relax.

My mother.

Wanted me to relax.

I should have been suspicious at the time. My mother wasn't the relaxing type of person, much less the kind of woman to encourage others to enjoy themselves. Least of all me. I took the bait, however, and went out for the evening with Tori. That's the night I met Kieffer, my next love interest and roller-coaster ride. I had fun that night, but at what cost I wouldn't discover until the next morning.

When I returned home with Tori the next morning, we found a Child Protective Services vehicle in the driveway. My mother had called them and told them I was out partying all night and left my son at home. She told them I did this pretty much every night, which was a lie. I tried to tell them she told me to go out, but they wouldn't listen. They gave my mother temporary custody in light of my actions. My mother had set me up and I had fallen hard for it.

To make matters worse, CPS threatened to put my son in foster care if I didn't sign custody of him over to my mom because I wasn't financially stable. I wanted to get a lawyer to fight it, but I couldn't afford one. I felt like a frightened animal backed into a corner. I didn't know what to do. I didn't want to give over custody of my son, but I didn't want to risk losing him forever to a strange family. So I did what I thought was the right thing. I signed over temporary custody of my child to my mother. I would go back to school and get a job and a place of my own and within a year I would prove I could take care of him. I would get him back and I would be a great single mom.

I heard a saying once that hindsight is twenty-twenty. That means when you look back on something you see what was happening with such clarity it seems so obvious what you should have done. What I should have done. Why am I always thinking about what I should have done? Again, I find myself cringing at the choices I made. I did what was best for my son at the time, but I didn't follow through with my plan. I didn't get a steady job, or finish college, or get a place on my own. I fell into another abusive relationship with another asshole and lost myself in the process.

My relationship with Kieffer was complicated and dangerous. It was also well documented on the *Teen Mom 2* series, which is why I am not going to dwell on it here. I will talk about how he led to my first arrest, because it was my trouble with the law that eventually led me to the Zebra Diary.

In October of 2010, Kieffer and I needed a place to stay. He knew a guy with a family who owned a beach house in Oak Island. The family was away for the off season so it was the perfect place for us to crash while we got our shit together. Neither of us could find work and we had no money and now I had lost my son. Things were looking desperate. So I agreed to stay at the house for a few days. A few days turned into a few weeks and one day the cops came along and threw us out. Apparently, we couldn't prove that our friend's grandmother said we could stay there so we had to go. We left.

We went back to the same house a few days later. I know! I know! Not the brightest move I've ever made, but our stuff was still there and we needed a place to stay. We had nowhere else to go. That night I got up to pee and a few moments after I flicked on the bathroom light, the cops started beating on the front door. They had been watching the house and said if I couldn't get ahold of our friend right then, they would arrest me. I couldn't, so they arrested me for breaking and entering and possession. (I had some pot and a pipe.) Then they began to ask the same question I had on my mind. Where was Kieffer?

I thought about it a moment and decided that he was probably down the street at another friend's house. The cops took me down there to find my car sitting in the driveway with the door standing open and the front door to the house standing open. I began to worry something was wrong with Kieffer. This looked bad. It was worse than I could've imagined. Kieffer got up in the middle of the night, leaving me alone, so he could go and party with his friends. I was so pissed off. The cops put him in the back of the patrol car with me, specifically instructing me not to scream at the guy. The officers knew me through my years of living on the island. They knew I would chew Kieffer a new one if given the chance. I was glad both of us were in handcuffs or I would've done something I would've regretted.

That was the first time we broke up. I told him not to talk to me. I plead guilty to the BnE and possession charges, and got twelve-month probation with monthly drug testing. This started us down that on-again, off-again relationship path. We would see each other for a little while, hook up a few times, then I would get over him again. I might've been a pot smoker, but I didn't really want someone around who was going to get involved in harder drugs. I had a hard enough time keeping Jace in my life as it was.

I always get sucked back into that rut where I self-identified through my relationship with a man. I could only find value in what he thought of me, or how others saw me when I was with him. Having a man on my arm made me feel stronger, like I could face anything. I suppose I used men as a shield against the world. Someone I could stand behind rather than stand with.

My obsession with Kieffer is what got me arrested the second time. I got into a fight with my friend Brittany over him. She was flirting with Kieffer, and my other friend (also named Brittany, oddly enough) pointed it out to me. I started questioning Brittany about it, which translates into me yelling and cussing at her because that's my natural reaction to any situation. The other Brittany egged me on and then physically pushed me into the first Brittany, which really started the fists flying. We fought while a good two dozen people stood in a circle watching us scratch and punch at each other. The fight didn't last long. Eventually we ran out of steam and the show was over so the crowd broke up.

It wasn't until a week later that I was arrested for it.

Someone in the crowd filmed the fight, then sold it to an online tabloid. Once the state saw the fight, they came and arrested all of us involved, including both Brittanys! We were all charged with assault and affray for fighting. I posted my own bond and got myself a lawyer fast. The trial wouldn't take place until later that year. On my lawyer's advice, I decided it was time to take care of myself. After all of the partying and running around and getting into trouble and chasing the ghost of satisfaction all over Oak Island, I needed to focus on getting well and finding myself.

The first step to this was checking myself into a rehab facility.

The Zebra Diary

Six days into my rehab I returned to my roots of keeping a journal of my experiences. I was at the Malibu Horizon facility in California. The first thing they did was take all of my electronics from me. That meant my phone and my laptop. So I sort of fell back into keeping a journal since I didn't have any other distractions. I will keep a day-to-day for a few weeks, then begin to slack off and quit for a while. These entries are long and detailed about my day-to-day experiences. Not a lot of drama here, mostly just me getting clean.

Day 6 @ Malibu   05|13|11
                        Friday

So today was fun. Well the end
of the day was. We got to go
shopping in target & tried to go
to the mall but it sucked. So
we go to this other huge one
and everything was closing :̈
BUT got everything I needed
at Target and saw Fabeo lol!
Earlier today I just worked on
this book called "Stop the Chaos"
and it's awesome and really helps
me to look at situations in a
different perspective. Malibu
is different from what I expected.
There are huge mountians and
valleys and it's not so much about
the beach. Earlier I made a
phone call to my mom and she
just yelled at me about going
to Target and she is opening
ALL my mail at home which
invades my privacy. It really
bothers me. Then she let me
talk to Jace on the phone for
2 minutes which REALLY upset
me. By the time I got off
the phone she made me

5/13/11

in tears and so crying so bad I couldn't catch my breath. I think she is afraid of me taking custody back and her being lonely the rest of her life. I feel as if she wants him to herself and replaced me with him. Which my anger isn't towards Jace at all because I know it's not his fault but I'm so mad at this point I'm going to disown her in my family. She is mean to everyone which isn't fair. She is bringing it all on herself. I'm so upset she shows no love cares for, or even show me affection and I love her so much I can't figure out why she is treating me like this when I'm staying positive and doing the right thing. Maybe she holds the past against me and doesn't believe I'll change. I can't go back to that toxic enviornment and I want my son back. I still haven't gotten over the fact that I don't have custody and she makes me pay child

5/13/11

support when we live together and I'm her daughter! I know it goes towards Jace but she gets money from Andrew, I mean $356 a month from him for Jace! I buy Jace things he needs all the time so I don't see the need to pay child support. Why is she so mean and yell at me when I'm going through such a hard time?! She doesn't even let me take care of him during the week when I'm free. She claims "he needs daycare." Why is she paying for daycare when his own mother can take care of him for free?! I mean I can't even express how upset she made me from a 2 minute phone call. And when I hungup she didn't even bother calling back to comfort me. Well after I cried one guy here named Tom seen me upset and talked me through and calmed me down to where I totally forgot why I was upset in the first place! Thank God someone cared. ☺

5/13/11

⟿ Tomorrow should be a better day. We are going on a hike to the "HOLLYWOOD" sign! I'm super excited. Then a movie later on that night. ☺ Other then that the doctors here are trying to figure out if I am bi-polar or not. If I am it won't hurt my feeling I will feel ~~relieve~~ relieved! Then I can get the medicine I need so I'm not always so moody. I'm figuring out lots of things about myself and my thinking process and IM SOBER! That makes me extremely happy. I want me and Jace to live a happy sober life and I will never treat him the way my mom treats me. I'm better then that. Especially with the cooping skills I'm learning I can hold my temper somewhat better but working on it. I got this book to jot down all my feelings while I'm going down this journey of recovery. Well its late so I'll write more tomorrow. Im just getting started. ☺

Jenelle Evans

This entry is a longer one, describing my impressions of the facility and the surrounding area. California was far different from I expected. Between the mountains on one side and the beaches on the other, it's sort of like the Carolinas. Just sunnier! The folks at the facility were really nice, and the other patients were kind to me. There were two houses for the patients, and we were spread between them. We did all kinds of things to help us move on from our addictions like art classes, group discussions, one-on-one sessions, and my favorite, equine therapy.

I really enjoyed my time at Malibu. I felt like it was an effective tool to help me get off and stay off of drugs. I only wished I had chosen to surround myself with people who also wanted to see me clean and sober for the rest of my life. But more on that later.

In this entry, you can see it doesn't take long for me to break down about my mother and my son. She is still withholding him from me. Using him against me like some tiny weapon. I don't understand why she wanted to hurt me when I was trying to do the right thing for him and myself. I just wanted to call and hear their voices, but she started yelling right away and wouldn't let me talk to Jace for more than a few minutes. I talk about disowning her and my entire family. It was hard to stay positive about my recovery when she was so negative.

Toward the end of the entry I began to talk about the possibility of being bipolar for the first time. This realization came as a kind of strange relief to me. Just the idea that I had a fixable problem and I wasn't just a fuck up made me feel all kinds of good. After my time in the media's eye, and all of the horrible judgments people made of me both online and in person, I began to think I was just broken inside. Broken and irreparable. I was a waste. I wasn't any good to anyone. I was nothing.

Then I found out I was fixable. How great was that? Through either therapy or chemistry, I was going to get better. I was going to get help.

I needed help, that's true, but it wasn't chemistry or therapy I needed. What I needed was understanding and guidance. I wasn't broken or a waste. I was a human being who made some bad choices and lived a complicated life. The folks at Malibu did their best to diagnose and treat me, but in truth I needed far more treatment than the staff could provide. I needed TLC.

I needed love.

Day 7   5/14/11
                               Saturday

So today started out fun. I
woke up and went to Hollywood
Blvd. and seen all the celebrities
hand prints and foot prints. :)
We also went and got some
suvinaurs from this shop. Then
I got back to the house and got
all my electronics back. That made
me extremely happy. Then I look
up my college courses online and it
said I wasn't registered for
anything which I def. was because
I did that a month ago. After
that I called my mom to have
a conversation with her with what
I've been up to and the first thing
she did was yell and yell and yell
at me. I'm DONE with this. I
told her I disowned her as a mom.
She told me she went through my
entire car and has been opening
my mail INCLUDING my bank
statements! I'm so angry, livid,
and upset. I've been crying for
30 minutes She is still sending
me nasty texts. On top of all of this
my sister sold ANOTHER

5/14/11

~ story to a magazine about my brother hitting her which was 2 years ago! Idk what to do since I'm all the way in California. ☹ Seems like my family replaced me with Jace and fame and fourtune. It hurts me so bad. Almost to the point of having a mental breakdown. She shows me no love, doesn't care, and doesn't give me ANY type of privacy. I feel so much more support from my ~~ friends and everyone here at this facility then I had in YEARS. Maybe cutting my family out of the picture will be a good thing for a couple years. I notice the only time I'm upset is when I'm talking to my mom. Even though my emotions are killing me right now I get through this and take one step at a time and be more successful then she EVER was and will be. ☺

Jenelle Evans

I make a realization in this entry that I should've seen a long time ago. I can see it easy when I read back on my diaries. I always get upset when I talk to my mother. I am feeling fine one moment, then I talk to my mom, and boom! I am pissed off. Talking to my mother should be a supportive check in. It should be a chance to say "hi" to her and my son and to hear about how everyone's life is back home. It never was. Talking with my mom was always a screaming match waiting to happen. There was never a time when I called her that she didn't start the conversation by complaining about something I had done, then launched into a screaming fit about it.

I talk a bit in this entry too about how my family has a tendency to sell articles about me and each other. God, I hate tabloids! They are always printing lies and bullshit about me and my family. It makes it so much more frustrating when one of my own family members actually sold the story to the tabloid. In this case, I am upset because my sister has sold a story about my brother hitting her. Like siblings never get into fights. Even as adults, brothers and sisters get into it over the littlest things. Why is this news? Why is that interesting to people? I just don't get it.

It wasn't just my sister either. My mother does interviews all of the time and of course has appeared alongside me both on 16 and Pregnant and Teen Mom 2. My sister sells articles any chance she can get. My dad—the same man who cut himself out of my fucking life when I was little—has even sold an interview to the press. He doesn't even know me! My brother, the one I thought I identified with the most, keeps a regular social media page where he posts all kinds of lies about me. It makes me feel a little sick inside when I think about all of them.

Here, I began to feel like my mom, sister, and brother had replaced me with money and fame and my son. They had my fame to launch their own stories. They didn't need me anymore. I felt so alone. All I wanted was my family to love me and respect me, but no. I didn't think they ever would. I am still not sure if they do.

The folks at the facility, including the other residents, were kind to me. The kindest anyone had been to me in a long time. I was pleased to be treated like a person for once, and not like a faceless celebrity, or a pregnant mistake, or a doormat girlfriend.

5/14/11

So the end of the day was good.
I didn't eat dinner but spent a lot
of time with the girls. We watched
No Strings Attached and now getting
ready for bed. I wanted to write
really quick because something very
funny just happened. One of the girl's
here came out of her bathroom
screaming "OMG. A MOUSE!" So me

and the nurses checked it out and
holy shit it was huge! lol, they
just put the mouse, that was on
the sticky pad, in a trash bag
and threw it away. It was so
funny, everyone was freaking out
but me, haha! Other then that
a new guy arrived at house 2
tonight so I'll meet him tomorrow.
And another girl + guy are coming
tomorrow. I'm looking foward to
meeting them. ☺ Well I'm going
to bed! so GOODNIGHT!

This short one is actually an extension from the previous entry. I thought it was funny so I included it here.

After we had dinner and watched a movie, one of the girls came out of the bathroom screaming about seeing a mouse. I went with the nurse to check it out and, yeah, there was a dead mouse on a glue trap. It was a big one, but the thing I remember most was how everyone else was freaking out about it, except for me. I watched quietly as they moved the dead mouse to a trash bag and got rid of it. I didn't understand what the big deal was.

Maybe the other people never saw mice growing up. I sure had. Not that my mother's homes were mouse riddled, but yeah, I had seen a few mice here and there. I certainly saw some in the places I had lived with Kieffer. I would see a lot later and write about it. Life was full of pests. Both of the rodent and human kind.

Day 8

5/15/11
Sunday

So today I woke up at 10am!
I slept 12 hours, lol. Then we went
out and seen Braidsmades. OMG!
It was SO funny and def worth
seeing. Before the movie we window
shopped @ some stores and I got
Jace the cutest motorcycle jacket.
I know he will love it. In the
morning I got a call from my
therapist saying my mom has
been calling the facility flipping
out. I have no idea why. I haven't
spoken to her since yesterday
afternoon. Weird :/. Other then
all of that I'm def in a good
mood. ☺ Just listening to music
in my room stress-free. Feels
AWESOME. Well I'll write later but
things are looking on the bright-
side for once.

You can see I am settling into the routine of life at the facility. This entry almost doesn't need an explanation. I was feeling pretty good, getting used to being in California, and doing day-to-day stuff. My mother had been calling the facility wanting to know why I was out instead of tied up to some bed. I think her idea of rehab was being locked in a room with no windows or friends or fun. She wanted punishment, not remedy.

I had gotten to where I would deliberately not talk to her so it wouldn't ruin my mood. I wanted to be happy, and not talking to my mom was part of that process. The only problem with that plan was it meant not talking to Jace either. Eventually I would have to suck it up and call her, just so I could get that possible few moments of hearing my son's voice.

If you notice, I am not writing about another thing here either, and my mood is great. That's right. I am not writing about boyfriends or lovers or abusers. I am focusing on myself and leaving all of that behind. Before, when I would write about just myself, I often talked about how I hated myself. But here, I was learning to love myself and leave all of those troublemakers behind me. I didn't need a guy to make me feel alive. I was alive.

Funny side note, I got Jace that motorcycle jacket at a pretty fancy boutique for kids. I often found myself buying him stuff he didn't need just to prove I was a good mother and could provide for him. I still have that jacket. After Jace outgrew it, I let my second son Kaiser wear it. I want to let little Ensley wear it but I think it's going to wear out before then. Even fancy things fall apart after so much use. Everything falls apart. Everything changes.

Day 9   5/16/11
                                        Monday

Today we went to equine therapy.
That was a lot of fun. We got to
train the horse to run in a circle
without using a rope and in an
areana. :) took lots of pics and
videos. My mood today is very
mellow. Not angry or moody and
simply happy. It's amazing
because it's only day 9! I'm also
very happy because I finished
my book! "Stop the Choas". Which
that book is amazing and really
helps in any person's recovery.
I just tried calling my mom to
speak to Jace but as usual
no answer. :(BUT it's not going to
ruin my day because I'll talk to
him eventually. I have been
attending groups and they help to
know I'm not the only one going
through these rough times. Well
I'll write later, a guest speaker
is here to talk then going to the
dentist @ 3:00pm. BYE!

                    Jenelle Evans

This was the day we started equine therapy. I love horses so this was a great day for me. Horses are always so majestic and powerful; I feel at such peace around them. I would love nothing more than to run and run and run, and never look back. That would be the best thing ever.

I also finished my workbook *Stop the Chaos*. It was a great tool to help me get my life together, and I recommend it to anyone in need of therapy. I wish I still had my copy of it so I can see the things I wrote at that time. I remember it being an emotional experience because it revealed things to me about myself that I never thought about. Things that had always been there, just under the surface, but I never saw. In fact, I made a list of those things. They are part of the Zebra Diary and I will share them with you here in a bit.

Calling my mother was a mistake, but I really wanted to talk to Jace. It had been a few days and I wanted to hear his voice. She never answered. Again, she was all about punishment. She had been punishing me since the day I told her I was pregnant with Jace. Even before that. Why would I think she had changed just because I was willing to change?

The best thing that happened to me at the facility was learning that I wasn't the only one going through those things. Group therapy taught me that other people suffered from the same things I did. Family difficulties. Addiction. Abuse. I had spent years thinking I was the only one, but I wasn't. Others suffered as I did. I was fucked up but I wasn't alone.

More importantly, I was pretty normal.

That meant everything to me.

Day 10   5/17/11
                          Tuesday

Right now I'm in group. I
started out with a good day by
going to the gym and getting a
good workout. Then I get back
and check facebook but I wanted
to call my mom, I just had a bad
feeling. So she tells me that she
absces on her breast and on her
tailbone and has to go into
immediate surgery and it's
making her very sick and she
started to cry and hungup on
me again. I hate that she
pushed me away again when I
was trying to comfort her. It
makes me so upset that I feel
like bawling in tears because I
noticed as the years go on she
is getting sicker and sicker and
getting more and more problems.
How is she going to take care of
Jace in this condition while I'm
gone and she is recovering? I'm
so worried it's unbelievable. I
feel like I have to leave but
I can't because I'm not finished
with the program. But

5/17/11

how can I focus on myself
while I'm in here if I'm worrying
about life at home. I don't
know. I need to talk to my thearpist
about this ASAP before I freak
out or have a nervous breakdown.
I say that because me and my
mom argue so much I'm afraid
it will still continue until she
dies and then I'll feel like it
was my fault we didn't try to
work things out. It scares me
with all these diseases popping
up because she might die early
before we clarify things. I'm
stuck. I don't want to be in group.
I want to cry and cry. UGH!
Why wouldn't she even call me
to mention this? Does she really
think I hate her THAT bad?
I need to let go and just talk
to someone. My craving to smoke
now is shooting through the
roof. I don't know. Talk more
later

Jenelle Evans

After a few days of not talking, I finally got ahold of my mother. She told me about a problem she was having with some abscesses and that she would need minor surgery. She hung up on me while crying, which of course freaked me out. She sounded like she was dying. I thought she might be, the way she was acting. In the end, she was panicking about a fairly run-of-the-mill surgery, though for her I am sure it was a big deal.

My takeaway from this was the understanding of my mother's mortality. The same woman who had custody of my son was herself getting older. If she were to pass away and still have custody of Jace, what would happen to him? Would those rights revert to me? Who would take care of him?

This started a chain reaction of wild, morbid thoughts. I didn't want to lose my mom. I mean, yeah, we fought like cats and dogs. But I didn't want her to die. Did I think she would be here forever? I think most kids do. We think our parents are immortal. It is a huge load suddenly dropped on your shoulders when you understand they are not immortal. Your parents will die one day. Then I got to thinking about my own mortality. Jace would even lose me one day.

From imitation leather jackets to moms, everything falls apart. Everything changes.

It made me want to call her and tell her I was sorry. I wanted to work things out before *it* happened. I wanted to take all the blame for our troubled relationship just to know we cleared the air between us. That moment passed eventually, and I came to grips with the fact that she was overreacting, and as a result so was I. My mother was still alive. This was just a minor surgery. She wasn't dying.

I don't think she deliberately worried me. I think she was having a little freak-out of her own and spread the panic my way accidentally. I am prone to overreacting and she knows it. I just happened to catch her at a bad moment, which spilled over to become my bad moment. The urge to smoke some weed became so overpowering. I don't know how I managed to avoid it. Other than the fact that I was in rehab and couldn't get ahold of any.

Thank heaven for small favors.

5/18/11
Wednesday

Day 11

Today we went for a workout again instead of the beach because the weather didn't look so good. Yesterday I stayed in my room for the rest of the day because I was really depressed about the bad news. Lunch was a mexican soup I didn't like so I didn't eat it. Dinner was mexican lagzona which I didn't like so I didn't eat it. After everyone heard I didn't eat and how upset I was they got me burger King. lol. Today though is going alright so far I'm in a good mood and tried to call my mom but no answer. Tried to text, no answer. I don't know what her deal is. But I'm not going to let it ruin my day. ☺ Well I'm going to talk to my therapist now so I'll check in later.

Janelle Evans

Day 11   5/18/11

Right now I'm in group and can't pay
attention because of my therapy session.
She told me they aren't going to cover
any of my health needs. So now
I'm in cronic pain with my jaw and
teeth and my back from giving birth
and having the epidural. They had to
stick me 4 times before they got it
in the right place. My mom and I are
doing a family session on Friday and
not looking forward to that. I haven't
even been eating. I'm so upset, so
depressed can't stop crying. I just
want to go home. Then move out
and start college. Kieffer called me
last night and we worked things
out but he hasn't called me all
day and I can't stop wondering
why. There I go not focusing on
myself. I need more places to go
and not be so bored as much.
If I don't I go crazy. I don't
know. It's whatever.

Jenelle Evans

I tried not to let the news about mom bother me, but I couldn't help it. The rest of that day the weather looked crappy, so I hung out in my room all day. I was so worried about my mother I couldn't eat. Both lunch and dinner were unappealing. I was in a funk and not sure how I would get out.

My friends at the facility saw how down I was, and that I wasn't interested in eating the offered meals. Some of them got together and bought me a meal from Burger King. How nice was that? This single act brought a smile to me. The next day I started feeling better. At least I did that morning when I woke up.

Later that day, I made a second entry. I just learned that the facility wasn't going to address my medical issues, which were many. I had jaw problems from a lifetime of carrying stress in my jaw. It would click and pop and ache for no reason. I also had a number of post-pregnancy issues and some other stuff I needed treatment for. Chronic pain is no joke.

Atop this I was worried about my upcoming family session with my mother in the next couple of days. I was back to not eating and crying all of the time. Maybe part of it was detoxing from the weed. Maybe part of it was that phone call with Kieffer.

Yeah, you read that right. I was talking to Kieffer again.

Funny how I was in a great mood until I talked to him. I can see that now, but then? Then I saw him as an escape from my current torture. He was an out for me. No. He was less of an out and more of an in, back to the life I was trying to get away from. He was dangerous to me. He was dangerous for me. A gateway back into the drugs and party life I was trying to leave behind. He would end up dragging me down further than I ever suspected I would go. And damn if I couldn't wait to leave the comfort of Malibu and get there.

5/19/11   Day 12
Thursday

So today started out great.
Went to the beach, even though it
was only 68°, we watched the
surfers. Then I got back and got
a hour full body massage and
tommorrow is gym day so I'm looking
forward to that. Other then all of
that I had steak w/ mac n'
cheese for lunch, and having
pasta for dinner! So everything
is working out smoothly today.
I started my Autobiography
assignment today and it starts
with childhood memories. I realized
I had a horrible childhood. :(
But at least I'm realizing how I
got to my problems that I have
today, so I'm looking foward to
doing more tomorrow. :) Well I
write later but I have to go to
a meeting. BYE!

Jenelle Evans

There are three words that can explain why Day 12 was so calm and serene when compared to the other days.

Full. Body. Massage.

I guess there are things that can relax you besides drugs. I know it is hard to sympathize with an addict when the whole rehab facility sounds like an excuse for a vacation. Horseback riding, once-a-week massages, shopping trips into town, and movie excursions. All of these things were meant to take our minds off of the various reasons we were there to being with. Like the massage, for example. It was meant to relax us and give us a chance to let our minds turn inward for a while.

And boy, did it work.

I started working on an autobiography too. Not the one you are holding. It was a more of a guided assignment that we were supposed to work on and turn in to our therapist. Kind of like an assignment for school, which, as you know, I excel at when I put my mind to it. It started out, of course, with our earliest childhood memories. That was when it hit me that I had a pretty shitty childhood. And not just that, but also how much of my crappy upbringing lead me here.

How old was I? Seriously? You would think I would've figured that one out a long time ago. But sometimes you don't really put the pieces together until you take the time to reflect on them. Writing it all down let me see where I had been, and where I was going. Sort of like this biography you're reading now. It's the end result of even more history and more years.

Writing it out started to give me some peace as well. I began to come to terms with my choices, both bad and good. My life, I realized, was a collection of decisions and results. I had made them all. Sure, some of them were influenced by others, but in the end I was responsible for them. I decided I was responsible for my own life, and I wouldn't let anyone else take charge of it again.

At least, I thought I wouldn't.

Day 13   5/20/11
                                          Friday

Okay, today started out with
the gym in the morning. I had a
very good workout. Then got back
to the house and changed clothes
and headed to the other house
for a group session. Ate lunch. Had
turkey and cheese sandwhich and
even ate two! I guess I was
really hungry, lol. Now I'm still
at the other house just chillin for
a bit until we head back. At 5pm
I have a family session with my
mom. Oh god, not looking foward
to that. So far on my autobiography I got 5 pages done. It
makes me happy how much
motivation I have to write that
much. As for me and Kieffer I
told him I'm not ready to be in
a relationship with him. He
hasn't changed as much as I
thought he did so back to focusing
on me. :) Later on we are going
to the mall so that will be fun.

Jenelle Grant

Another good day. You can see the day-to-day routine of journal writing gets a little tedious. It starts to become *I woke, I ate, I went back to bed.* Don't worry, my friend. The ride is about to get bumpy again here really quickly.

So that day I got more of my autobiography done, and was pleased with my progress on it. Writing my life story gave me something to focus on, but it also gave me something to achieve. A goal I could feel accomplished about once finished. It was nice to have something to feel good about for a change.

I don't write about my meeting with my mother that day, but that is probably because it wasn't something I wanted to dwell on. It went about as expected. My mother explained to the therapist how everything was my fault. I spent the time trying not to blow up at her, which left me tense and angry. The therapist was good about my mom. She tried to explain to the both of us how we each were responsible for our own portion of what was happening. She laid out our relationship as she saw it and made some suggestions for improving things between us.

My mother didn't listen to the therapist. And the funny thing was how mom kept repeating that I never listened. The therapist was trying to explain things but my mother wouldn't stop complaining long enough to hear anyone else. I think the therapist got a good impression of what I deal with every day. It's hard to listen to what someone is saying when all they do is scream at you.

I may have wanted to forget my meeting with my mother, but I made sure to write down what happened when I talked to Kieffer. I spoke with him and told him I was not ready to be in a relationship with him. He claimed he was different and getting his shit together, but no, I could tell he wasn't. He was the same old Kieffer. He would just tell me anything I wanted to hear to get me back. Not this time, I told myself. This time I was focusing on Jenelle. Enough of giving my heart away to someone who wouldn't respect it.

I thought I was done with him and ready to move on.

Day 14   05|21|11
Saturday

⟶ Today started out sucky.
We went to the beach and it was
foggy. ☹ But we left early so I
could tan on our front porch
because it was hot + sunny. We
ate lunch outside, got a tan, life
felt great. I felt so peaceful.
Then we had Art Therapy. They
told us to use any materials
we wanted to to show how we
were feeling today. So I made
a landscape of the beach and
ocean. I did that because I
felt really relaxed and calm
today. I sware each day here
gets easier and easier. ☺ I'm
excited to go home even though
I'm only half way through. For
dinner I had a steak and a
twice baked potato. It was
AWESOME! Then I called my
mom and Jace and talked to
Jace for a good few minutes.
So today ran smoothly. I did
have a bump in the road
which was logging onto facebook
and seen Kieffer was already

Day 14
05/21/11

in another relationship. When
I seen this I broke out in tears.
I was so upset. I was bawling
my eyes out and realize I cannot
lose him. So I called him and
we been talking all night and
worked things out. This is it.
No more breaking up and if we
break up it will be forever. No
more going back and forth. We
just got to talk about our problems
instead of breaking up every time.
I'm hurt by him being able to
have freedom while I'm stuck here
and can't do shit. But about that
relationship he was in it was
fake to hurt my feelings. Which it
worked and I honestly thought
it wouldn't hurt my feelings to
hear he was in another
relationship but I realized I
have too much love to let him
go. I don't care what anyone
else thinks either. ☺

Janelle Evans

Really? I thought I was done with Kieffer. I swear I did!

Okay, so the day started pretty good, with the art therapy. I have always been a creative person, so getting the chance to express myself is great. It was only natural that I chose the beach as a subject for feeling calm and relaxed. I've always associated the beach with calmness. Ever since my family moved to Oak Island, and my young life improved, I've connected the ocean with contentment.

The day was even smooth after talking to my mother, which is a surprise in itself. Maybe she really did listen to the therapist after all. Who knows? She let me speak to Jace and the whole thing didn't end in yet another screaming match. Any time I can talk to my mother with minimal yelling is a good experience.

Speaking of screaming, let's get back to the Kieffer thing. What in the hell was I thinking? Now I can see what an absolute lovesick fool I was. One day I say I am done and the next I am begging him to take me back. Ugh. It turned out that much like my experience with drugs, it would take nearly dying to get me off of Kieffer for good.

So there I am, having a splendid day. I got to create. I got to talk to my son. I managed to navigate a conversation with my mom without it ending in World War Three. Life was good.

Then, Facebook.

That should be a t-shirt. Seriously. *Then, Facebook.* How many times has a moment of joy flipped like a coin into sorrow simply because of something you saw on social media? *Then, Facebook.* I swear it's the story of my entire life. If it isn't Facebook, it's something else online, or in magazines, or on the television. Every time I turn around I feel like some form of media is calling me out, or judging me, or telling me how to live my life. It makes you wonder why you bother with social media. I guess it's just like any other addiction. You get highs and lows from it. You take the good with the bad.

In this case, I saw a post by Kieffer on Facebook that turned my mood from sweet to sour in an instant. It wasn't even a post, really. It was that little change announcement that shows up in your friends' feeds so they can see what is happening in your life. His was a simple change. He went from not seeing anyone to in a relationship. In a relationship? Wait a minute. Didn't I just tell him yesterday that I didn't want to see him anymore? I realize I had cut him free, but it wasn't even twenty-four hours later and he was already in a relationship?

I panicked. My mind immediately went to a dark place. There was only one answer. He was seeing someone on the side while he was supposedly waiting for me to get back from rehab. This realization made me feel sick. I burst into tears and cried for a good hour about it. Then I broke down and called him. I needed to confront him and find out the truth about this new relationship of his.

Apparently, he had made the whole thing up to make me jealous. Well, it worked! I spent hours on the phone with him that night, working things out. God, reading that back makes me want to laugh out loud. Working things out meant we would get back together and—in my fantasy world—we would stay together forever because Kieffer was the perfect guy for me. (What was I thinking? I can't say that enough!) More importantly, I had decided that we would stop breaking up over fights. The next time we had an argument, we would talk it out and get over it and stay together. And if we decided to break up again, it would be forever. But we wouldn't break up because we were going to work it out forever and ever and ever. Yeah, because life is just that simple.

I think part of what was influencing my actions here was my frequent visits to therapists. I think I sort of got bit by that therapy bug, and thought I could talk out all of my problems. Certainly, if I could get through a family session with my mother I could talk things out with my boyfriend? Of course. Because, again, life is that simple.

We all know that life is not that easy. Toxic relationships only end up poisoning you. It's like the late stages of some tricky disease. You think you're getting better but in reality, you're just moving to a whole new level of fucked up. This is what would eventually happen between Kieffer and me. He would take me to places that I never thought I would go, and I would do things there I never thought I would do. It wasn't a good relationship. It was poisoning me.

At first figuratively, then later literally.

I have to laugh, too, at how I talk about how much love I have for him. I should really go back and count how many times I had *so much love* for my current boyfriend. There I am again, giving away too much to someone who doesn't really care about me. It would take a long time for me to learn to cut that shit out. A long time and a few more boyfriends I would have *so much love* for.

Day 15   05/22/11
Sunday

⤚ Today started out great I
woke up @ 10am and got ready
and we went out for lunch and
then went bowling. ☺ But the
entire time I was gone Kieffer
didn't call me once. So I called all
of his friends and they all said
they haven't seen him. So I waited
and waited. Then I get online
around 4:30pm and that girl
that Kieffer "faked" a relationship
messaged me and we started to
talk. Well come to find out he
played me. He told her to go down
from PA to NC ~~✗~~ and he would
rent a hotel room and they would
see how things went then get into
a relationship. Then as me and
her are talking he got online. I
was bawling my eyes out and I
started to cuss him out. All he
had to say was "I tried, bye"
and signed offline and I haven't
heard from him since. I can't
believe he did this to me. It
tears me apart. I knew I had
a bad feeling. ☹ Oh well,

05/22/11

that's the end of us and the start to my new life when I get home. ☺ Kinda happy it happened now because I would of beat the shit out of him if I was home, lol. Well I'm all better now. MTV will be here to morrow & I have equine therapy with the horses so that will be fun. CANT WAIT! But yeah guess I'm starting out fresh for the 100th time, lol.

Jenelle Evans

Oh what a difference a day makes. I should've stuck with my initial suspicions about Kieffer and his sudden relationship. Turned out I was right the first time. He had played me. He was talking to this supposedly fake girl the whole time I was in rehab.

I was worried because, after talking to Kieffer all night, he didn't bother to message me or call me the next day. I tried to contact him, and even called and messaged around looking for him, but all of his friends said they hadn't seen him that day. I ended up getting a message from a girl later that afternoon who introduced herself as being Kieffer's new relationship.

She reached out to me because she suspected Kieffer was still seeing me on the side and she wanted to find out before she traveled down from Pennsylvania to see him. That's right. Kieffer told her to come down to North Carolina and he would get her a hotel room and they would see how things went before they started getting involved in a relationship. This was such a blow to me. I felt like I had been hit in the gut. This was the same man who spent all night telling me how he had faked the relationship just to make me jealous and how much he really loved me. (Did I say man? I think I meant little boy!) How could he betray me like that? If he had told me the truth, maybe we could've worked it out. Maybe. It was the lying I couldn't take. I could withstand a great deal of torment from those around me, but I couldn't stand being lied to. I knew the girl was speaking the truth because she knew more things about Kieffer than just a casual friend should.

Especially a female friend.

I was devastated, again, to say the least. I started crying and got all worked up about it just in time for Kieffer to sign online. The moment I saw him pop up as available, I wrote him, slamming him for betraying my trust and talking to this girl behind my back, then lying about all of it. All the bastard had to say was, "I tried. Bye." And he signed out. That was that. That alone should've screamed about how guilty he was. He didn't get on and try to defend himself, or discount the other girl, or better still, he didn't hang around to apologize for his actions. Actions he knew were tearing me up inside. I was gutted, and he didn't care. That alone should have been a big, fucking clue that another attempt at a relationship would end in disaster.

I didn't hear from him for the rest of the night. Which was just as well because I didn't want to talk to him. I wanted to... well it's probably not best to say the thing I wanted to do to him. Let's just say they weren't pleasant. I wrote that I wanted to beat the shit out of him, but it went far deeper than that. The kinds of things I wanted to do weren't the kinds of things you do to a man you have so much love for either. That was the end of us. For today.

I wanted to get over him and get on with my life, but he would keep coming up again, like a bad penny, over and over. I would spend far too much of my precious time making him a priority when I should've been shuffling him to the curb, along with all of his baggage.

05/24/11
Day 17

Tuesday

Yesterday I didn't write but I was filming most of the day and I went to see the ~~horses~~ horses in the stables. That was fun as usual. Other then that I was really fucking irritated all day and couldn't figure out why. Well at the end of the day I started my period, lol. So I was PMSing I guess. Today I went to the gym and had a great workout. My autobiography is going well. I have 10 pages done! So I printed out what I had and gave it to my therapist. I'm suppose to go to group right now but I'm exhausted and I hate the other house. It's so dark and cold. Me and Kieffer are still over Andrew called me yesterday. We had a civil convo and he looks like he is getting his life on track. He claims he doesn't drink no more but Idk I'll only believe it when I see it. lol.

Jenelle Evans

See, I went a whole two days without getting back together with Kieffer! I was ready for my new life without him. I got back to my autobiography, finishing it, and even spent a day filming for the show without him on my mind. I didn't call him. I didn't text him. I was over him.

Andrew called me, which was an interesting conversation. He was polite and told me about how he was also getting his life on track. I guess he felt like he had to because he was talking to me in rehab. He told me he had stopped drinking, but I doubted it. And yeah, I was right; he still does now. Ah well, old habits are hard to break.

I would learn this soon enough.

05/25/11
Day 18

Wednesday

Today I was very upset and depressed.
Last night I watched 16 & P about
the anrexoxic girl and it made me
turn it off and go to my room +
cry my eyes out. Just seeing her
tiny baby made me think of Jace
when he was that small and I
never got to get the chance to
even take care of him because my
mom just took over. So I ended up
calling Keffer @ 1am his time
and he talked to me for an hour
and he calmed me down. For that
happening I realized I do
want to be with him. I love
him. So we are back together, lol.
For good this time. I sware! But
other then that next week is my
last week here! I'm so happy! I
get to go home, see Jace, see Cali,
drive my car, go to the beach, see
Keffer, AND MOVE OUT! I'm
very happy.

Jenelle Evans

Again? Back together again? I love him again? Why wasn't I taking notes?

Oh wait! I was! Then why didn't I read them in the next few days?

Who the heck knows why we do the things we do. Emily Dickenson said it best: The heart wants what it wants, or else it does not care. This means when the heart has itself set on a goal, nothing will stop it from gaining its goal. No betrayal, no sorrow, no level of soul searing pain would stand in the way of the possibility of love. Which was what my heart always wanted.

This little chain reaction was touched off, ironically enough, by an episode of *16 and Pregnant*. When I saw the baby, I found myself thinking back to when Jace was born. When he was so small and needed me, and I didn't get a chance to take care of him. How my mother took him away from me immediately. I broke down in tears and shut myself off in my room. I knew I needed to talk to someone about it, but I didn't have a whole lot of people I could call.

So I called him.

Kieffer calmed me down and talked me back to a place where I could think straight. That was Kieffer's gift. He could talk the birds down from the trees. He was charming when he wanted to be. I just wished his charm was bigger than his ego. Though then I obviously thought this charm was the best part of him, because I fell all the way for it. We were officially back together. Again. For the millionth time.

I was super happy to be going home soon, and super happy to be going there to see Jace, my family, and, of course, my man.

One more week and I would be back into the same old routine.

November 3rd, 2011

So I'm on stickam and talking to fans having a great time. My fans make me so happy they say positive feed back that no one can replace.

DONE!

Jennette pero

Conner's

I am sure you noticed there is a leap of time here. From May to November. I made one more entry before I was released from rehab, but it wasn't so much a diary entry as it was a list. I have included it here, after the Zebra Diary is done. I wanted to go over the rest of my story before we jumped into the conclusions of my weeks of therapy. (Which turned out to be wrong anyways.)

First, remember that brawl I had with Brittany back in March? Well we went to court in September over it. And I mean everyone went to court. Both of the Brittanys and me. After the judge watched the video and we each explained our side of the story, the ruling came down. The judge dropped the assault charges, thank goodness. Instead, all of us were charged with simple affray, which is basically fighting in public. There are only a few states that even have that as a charge, North Carolina being one of them. Go figure. We each got thirty days, suspended, twelve months supervised probation, twenty-four hours of community service, and last but not least we had to complete an anger management class.

I was happy with the ruling. I am glad the judge saw it was a provoked fight and not just me attacking Brittany for no reason. I haven't been in many fights in my life. Sure, I can scream with the best of them, yet I don't like settling things with fists. It leads to nothing but trouble.

And back to the diary entry, trouble was waiting for me as soon as I got out of rehab. Kieffer was in New Jersey, basically hiding from the police. He wanted to come and see me when I got out of rehab, so he risked the trip to North Carolina. While he was down, I encouraged him to turn himself in and face his responsibilities. He did, and ended up in jail for a while. This gave me a chance to cut Kieffer out of my life for good. He was away from me, which was a good start. As long as I had no way to contact him, I knew I could move past him.

I ended up moving in with one of my girlfriends. We got along well, and living with her was easy, at first. She introduced me to Gary, a sexy Marine who would soon become my next big thing. It seems I got over Kieffer long enough to fall in love with someone else. Though, Kieffer wasn't entirely out of my life just yet. I also got involved with another guy during this time, but not in a dating kind of way.

At the bottom of the diary entry you will see that I signed it as *at Conner's*. Conner was a friend of my friends. I don't know how he got into my circle of contacts or where he came from. He was sort of just there one day. While I was living with my friend, I heard through the grapevine that he needed a personal assistant. I was taking a break from the MTV filming, so I needed the work. I took the job, though I would regret it for the rest of my life.

Conner needed someone who could drive because, for unexplained reasons, he couldn't get a North Carolina license. He made and sold custom exotic wooden guitar necks online, and it was my job to package them and ship them off. It was easy enough, and Conner seemed like a nice guy. He was real friendly and funny. He loved to talk and joke around. He even offered me a place to stay, like a live-in assistant, but I was rooming with my friend Hannah at the time so I didn't need to stay with him. He was nice to my friends, too, and let Tori come and sit with me at work all of the time.

Truthfully, though, I started asking her to come to work with me because I began to get a creepy vibe from Conner. Like he wanted me to handle a different kind of package, if you get my meaning. He started hitting on me pretty heavily and in a couple of weeks he asked me to dinner one night. I showed up with Tori, which obviously disappointed him. The next day when I came in, he said I had to start dating him or I could find another job. I don't remember exactly what I said, but I think it was along the lines of fuck off, and I quit.

I wished that was the end of it, but no, it goes on and on and on.

Gary and I started dating by the beginning of 2012 and of course I fell hard for him. By this time, we had moved into a condo together because things were not working out between my friend and me. While I was having it out with Conner, I was also having it out with her. She had started spreading these terrible rumors about me as well. She kept telling people that Tori was a bad influence on me and that I should only be her friend. I began to see that she was more of a fan than a real friend. We got into a big fight about it and I asked her to move out. I ended up moving out from her place and into a condo with Gary.

My friend, on the other hand, moved in with Conner. Yeah, I know. Even though we had spat some serious venom at each other, when I found out about this, I tried to warn her about how sketchy Conner was. She wouldn't listen. She took the job I had as well as the offered room. I worried for her, even though I was super pissed at her for being such a bitch to me.

After a few days of working for him, Conner convinced her to take out a no-contact order on me for allegedly saying I was going to find her and beat her ass. By the time that went to court, she had already seen the real Conner and dropped the charges. I don't know exactly what he did to her to change her mind about him. Soon after, she moved out of Conner's house. I haven't talked to her much since.

Conner continued to harass me online, and spread rumors that I had slept with him. I never did. I will confess to once thinking that I had to use sex as a means to keep the man in my life happy, but Conner was never my man.

He was a boss at best, and an asshole at worst. And to tell the truth, I can do, and have done, much better than the likes of Conner. What in the world would make him think I would want to sleep with him?

Meanwhile, things were seriously heating up between Gary and I. We were in that golden hour of our relationship, when he could do no wrong and I believed every word that dropped from his lips. That didn't last long. Gary had a lot of anger issues and my history of taking such abuse lead to a dangerous mix. We started getting into fights about any little thing. He even proposed to me once during an argument!

I will never forget that moment. We had been fussing about something and he stormed out of the house as mad as a hornet. He was gone for a little while. I didn't care where he went, as long as I didn't have to see him. I was that mad at him. When he returned, he breezed into the house, dropped to one knee, and presented me with a ring. Seriously. The man had gone out and bought a ring while I was pissed off at him.

I took the ring at first, because it was a nice gesture. Later on, I thought about it and decided this wasn't what I wanted. I didn't want to build a marriage out of an argument. I gave it back to him and told him I couldn't accept it. Not yet. Two weeks later he proposed properly and I accepted, though we would never have a wedding day. We dated maybe six or seven months total. We were on again, off again, just like every other guy I have ever dated. All the while we fought about everything. I guess I was so used to fucked up relationships I was willing to put up with his short fuse just to have someone in my life. All of that came to an end when he finally snapped and laid hands on me during an argument.

Screaming matches I can take. Nearly choking the life out of me I will not.

It happened one night when he wanted to go out partying, and I wanted to stay home. This was the beginning of the end. He insisted that he could go anywhere any time he wanted, and I reminded him that while I didn't own him, he was my fiancé. Why would you want to go to a dance club and party all night but leave your lady home alone? There is only one answer to that.

You are seeing another woman. Or in his case, other *women*.

Of course, he went out on his own. I couldn't stop him, physically or verbally. I was upset and worried and mad at him about the whole thing. I hurled curses at him, but he left, eager to satisfy some urge to drink in the nightlife. I didn't go after him. I tried not to think the worst. I sat on my hands, telling myself he just wanted to blow off some steam. Even though he was going to a club full of hot young girls, I could trust him. I was the only woman in his life. Right?

I ended up calling him a few hours later to check up on him. Or check in on him. Any way you look at it, he was acting suspicious. Low and behold, a young woman answered his phone. I pushed down my anger and asked to speak to Gary. She just laughed and hung up. That was enough to set me off. I didn't have to look for him, I knew exactly what club he went to because the bastard told me before he left.

So, I went after him.

I found him at the club, hanging out and talking with a whole bunch of different girls like he wasn't engaged to someone already. I confronted him right there, in front of the woman he was hitting on. We got into a huge argument there in the club, screaming louder than the music, getting kicked out in the process. We went home, in separate cars, and didn't say anything else to each other for the rest of the night. We went to sleep angry, turning away from one another as we shared the bed.

Except I couldn't sleep. How could I? Boy, he sure didn't have trouble getting his nap on. He was dead to the world while I lay awake wondering how long this had been going on. Was this the first time he had cheated on me, or at least tried? Eventually, I got out of bed, found his phone, and I went through his texts and calls. Sure enough, there were calls to other women, and texts inviting them back to his house.

Our house.

That old familiar punched in the gut feeling came over me. This was the man I planned on marrying. How could he do this to me? Why was I always falling for such crap! Did I have a huge please-screw-me-over sign on my forehead? I sat there in the dark with the phone, crying silently to myself. I don't know how long I stayed like that, reading each text over and over, weeping quietly in the soft glow of the cell phone, while he slept on beside me in cheating bliss.

In time, he woke up and found me with his phone. I thought his head was going to explode right then and there. He wanted to know what in the hell I thought I was doing with his private property. I asked him what in the hell he thought he was doing inviting women back to our house. He said it was his house and that tipped us into another screaming match. We fought, hurling curses and verbal abuse at one another. I demanded to know how long this had been going on and he kept screaming about me violating his privacy by looking at his phone. He grabbed my phone and threw it against the wall, destroying it and with it my chance of calling my friends or family for help. I sank to the floor and started to cry.

He started screaming at me and I kept on crying. He was yelling at me to stop crying because the neighbors would hear. Yeah, like my crying is what they would hear and not his hollering at me? Things escalated pretty quickly after that, and next thing I knew, I couldn't breathe.

Gary had attacked me. He jumped up from the bed, looped his blanket around my throat, and pulled it tight. He kept screaming at me to stop crying while choking me all the while. I tried to fight back but I was lost. He was stronger than me, bigger than me, and had far more experience fighting than I did. Just when I thought I was going to pass out, or even outright die, he finally released me. Probably because I stopped crying. It's hard to cry when you can't breathe.

I immediately turned on him in self-defense. I wouldn't let him get me in that position again. I jumped onto the bed where he sat and punched him in the back. It was the only blow I got in, because he started to wale on me after that. He said if I was going to hit him like a full-grown man, he would hit back like a full-grown man. He punched me over and over and over. I ended up with bruises everywhere. I don't know how long he would've gone on hitting me if the police hadn't arrived.

Our earlier arguing had been loud enough to wake the neighbors, who in turn called the police. They showed up just in the nick of time. Gary released his hold on me and went to answer the door. When the police saw what was going on, a domestic dispute, they arrested both of us. I have never been so glad to see the police, even if they were hauling me off to jail. At least I wasn't dead at the hands of my angry fiancé.

Make that ex-fiancé. I let Gary go after that outburst. Again, I can take most of what anyone can throw at me emotionally, but I am not a punching bag. Believe it or not, he made a few death threats toward me after that. He said if I made a big deal out of what happened and got him kicked out of the Marines, he would kill me. This is the same guy for whom I bought an AK-47 on his birthday.

Yeah, I nearly married that.

Was I scared? You bet your life I was. I took out a no-contact order on him and that's the last time I talked to Gary. And for the gazzillionth time I was done being a doormat. How long did that last? Not long enough.

During all of this excitement, Kieffer got out of jail and was back in town. Yeah, we kept in contact even while I was dating Gary. I couldn't help it. Kieffer had seen me through some pretty dark times. I couldn't cut him out of my life entirely. We had too much history. Oh, I would learn just what it would take to cut that fucker out of my life for good soon. But then, we were still friends even if I was with another guy.

Here's the weird thing. Kieffer moved in with, of all people, Conner! What the ever-loving-fuck was up with that? He said he needed work and a place to stay, and Conner was the only place where he could find both.

Kieffer took the job both my old roommate and I escaped from. I was kind of surprised Conner would hire a man for the job, considering he was using the position as an excuse to get women into his bed.

After I thought about this for a bit, it became increasingly obvious exactly why he had hired Kieffer and let the man move in. He wanted to get more dirt on me. Conner was still harassing me online, Tweeting about me, and posting stuff all over the internet about me and my life. He kept insisting that I was sleeping with him, even though I was with Gary. I told Kieffer about this, and he said he knew Conner was a scumbag. He didn't really like Conner, but he needed money and a place to stay. Why not take advantage of the scumbag?

That was a good point. Kieffer lived with Conner for a couple of weeks. During this time, when Gary and I had broken up, I went to check on Kieffer. Yeah, I know, I am pretty dumb for willingly walking into Conner's house with everything that was going on between us online. I was there to see Kieffer and nothing more.

One thing lead to another between Kieffer and me. Old flames flickered, and next thing I knew, I had spent the night. The next morning, we went out to get some breakfast. When we got back to Conner's, all of Kieffer's things were on the porch. Conner had fired him and kicked him out. Why? Because of me. Conner was so obsessed with me he couldn't stand the thought of me with another man.

Kieffer found another place to stay, but we didn't pursue our relationship. I ended up back with Gary again, as his fiancé. And you know how that went.

Later I found out the real reason Conner couldn't get a North Carolina driver license. He was charged with domestic dispute in California, and reckless endangerment in New York. He was also behind on child support and on the run from the law. What an asshole! The cops came around and asked me a bunch of questions about him. I hope they nail him to the wall for the way he treats me and other women. I also hope he learns that what goes around, comes around.

09/10/12

Lots has happened since we last spoke. Kieffer & I got back together but last night he seen a fb message from another guy. Yes I did flirt to make Kieffer jealous so he can realize how mean he has been being to me. I took the convo too much too far and lead the guy on and now Kieffer thinks I was actually into him for calling him "gorgeous" Which is Kieffer's nickname I call him. Gary is long gone and I have a no-contact order out on him. Kieffer wants to leave me now. I have no idea what to do. My family I disowned, haven't seen Jace in 3 weeks, and no friends no support BUT Kieffer. I CAN'T lose him. He means the universe to me but he thinks I'm lying. I wish he would believe me. We were planning on

having a child & get
married and live a happy
life but now seems like
I ruined that, like always.
He is leaving today @ 4pm

I don't know how I'm
going to handle this. I'm
losing it. As soon as I hear
those words "It's over, for
good." I break down in tears.
& can't handle to even bear
to hear those words.

I guess we will see what
happens. I love you to
death Kieffer Charles
Alexander Delp I want to
be Mrs. Delp someday with a
child that reminds me exactly
of you.

Tune in later today.....

Another jump in time, ahead nearly a year. Everything I just described happened between the November entry and this entry. So by this time I am back with Kieffer again. Things are going about as expected. All he wants to do is smoke weed and lie around. I am back to my old habits of following his lead. We smoke, we bum around. Oh, and we shoot up.

Kieffer started using heroin at a young age. He was turned out of his house and had to live on the streets for a few years. In that time he started shooting up to escape the hardships of his life. He always had the habit. I figured it out when we first started dating. I would see him dip into a bathroom and come out with a grin on his face. He would be gone for a little while, then return in a far better mood. When I confronted him he said he didn't do it often, and I didn't have to know about it. I told him to keep me out of it.

The trouble was, I didn't want him in it either. I liked smoking weed every now and again, but I wasn't interested in getting involved in harder drugs. It bothered me that Kieffer thought he needed to go there. Wasn't my love enough to make him happy? Apparently not.

Then the inevitable happened. One afternoon through some magic of his double talk, Kieffer convinced me to give it a try. I said yes. It would be a yes I would regret to this day. I liked to take risks and I loved dangerous things. I also figured he wouldn't let me do something that would harm me. He loved me. Right?

My first trip was amazing. I won't glamorize the drug by going into the long details of why people love it so damned much. All I will say is Kieffer was right: it did make me feel good. Good enough to give it another go. And another. And another. Before I knew it, I was shooting up four or five times a day. I was hooked.

The first thing I lost to the drug was my family. I disowned my mother and siblings and friends, but the truth is no one wants to talk to you when they suspect you're a junkie. My mother wouldn't let me see Jace anymore so I made a big deal about not seeing her. Like it was my idea. It hurt my heart, made me sick to my soul that I couldn't see my son. I filled that hateful void with more drugs. The drugs always made the pain go away. They didn't turn on me or betray me. I guess heroin was my first steady, dependable lover. It gave me what I needed to live and I gave it my life.

By this entry, heroin was the only thing I had in my life that loved me. Kieffer was mad at me for flirting with some guy online. I felt like he was losing interest in me, so I concocted a plan to make him jealous. Stupid, I know, but it made sense at the time. Doesn't it always? I started messaging this guy and flirted with him, making sure to leave the messages open for Kieffer to see.

Kieffer did see, and he got pissed off. He read the messages, and said I went too far by calling the guy gorgeous. That was my nickname for Kieffer. What was I thinking? No wonder Kieffer got so angry. He ranted and raved about how I flirt with every guy. He started bringing up all of my past relationships, and arguing with me about whether or not I loved him. Then he said he wanted to leave.

"It's over for good," he said.

Those words broke my heart. I could hear them echoing in my head. It's over for good. He couldn't mean it. He didn't really want to leave, did he? He couldn't leave me! I was living with Kieffer then. I had no contact with my friends, my family, my son. I had no support network. I had no one else in my life but Kieffer. I needed him. We had just talked about getting married and having kids and everything that goes with it.

But I ruined it. All of it.

Kieffer was my world and I chased him away.

9/11/12

I'm super upset. I woke up to being accused of stealing. I started crying and admitted I stole from him. I did it because he took my phone. I want to be the only girl his calls Mrs. Dep. Not 5 years down the road and find out there is a tottally pretteier & smarter & has everything I didn't have. Now he is using my phone which is making me nervous. He tells me if he gets to use the phone he won't leave me, I' dont believe him. I'm torn apart. I hope & pray to God he stays with me. I can't stand him without him in my life. He is so mad @ me he just doesnt care. I feel as if I have no one I need to run far away. I betrayed Kieffer and I understand I'm the fuck up in this relationship not him, he is mean to me but I'm not giving him enough time to change.

He is calling everyone on my phone and I know he is trying to setup a ride to leave me ~~please~~ for good. I don't know what I'll do without my best friend, lover, partner in crime and comedian all in one he hates me to death just like everyone else.

God for once, help me.

Jenelle Evans

This next to last entry is one day later. Things are not any better. Kieffer is still pissed off at me. He's accused me of stealing. I would confess to anything he said I did because I was so desperate to keep him in my life. I want to be the only Mrs. Delp. I wanted to be the only one he ever loved, ever again. I was pretty pathetic.

Between his manipulation and the heroin, I sank low, so low. To one of the lowest points in my life. I glance back on these diaries and see myself at thirteen again, hating my mother for grounding me and taking everything from me, and leaving me alone to wish I was dead. Then I see myself at nearly twenty, with my boyfriend taking everything from me and leaving me alone to feel exactly the same way. I even begged God to help me. Everyone always left me. Even the drugs would leave me if I didn't keep taking them.

At one point, I waited too long between hits and began to come down from the heroin. I got sick, the sickest I had ever been. Kieffer explained that's what happened when you detoxed from the stuff. I wished he had told me that ahead of time; I would've never started taking it! I hurried to fill my body with more of it so the feeling would stop, and Kieffer helped give it to me. I thought he did it out of love. Now, I am sure he just wanted me to foot the bill.

Which is why we ended up moving to New Jersey. I don't really remember how it came up in our argument. One minute Kieffer was calling for a ride back home to get away from me, and next thing I know he was talking me into moving there with him. Yes, I said. Another yes I would come to regret. What a great idea, right? I already miss my friends and family when they are just down the road from me. Why not pick up and move hundreds of miles away from them so I can't see them at all? I wasn't thinking about any of them. I was only thinking about Kieffer. He was my knight on a white horse, rescuing me from my awful life. Well, the horse was white, but he was no knight.

We rode that horse all the way to New Jersey, where it nearly killed me.

We moved up north and stayed with his mom for a while, sleeping on an air mattress while I looked for a place to rent. I don't think I even told my mother we were moving up there. I just picked up and left. We stayed in New Jersey together for about a week. Over that time, I did a lot of heroin and weed. That was all I did. Just smoked and shot up and laid around chillin'. We hid it from his mother and his friends, which isn't easy to do when you are strung out. About a week into it, I woke up on the bathroom floor after a blackout. I had no idea how long I was out or what I did during that time. It was scary, not knowing. Just losing a chunk of time like that.

I asked Kieffer why I was lying on the fucking floor. Kieffer said I passed out. I asked why they didn't take me to the hospital. Kieffer's response was so casual, I nearly choked on his words.

"Sometimes that just happens," Kieffer said.

"What the fuck do you mean?" I said.

"Sometimes that just happens," he said again.

He meant that it was just a thing that happened on heroin. Sometimes you just black out. Sometimes you lie around on the bathroom floor while your boyfriend enjoys his high. Sometimes you wake up wondering what just happened. Sometimes you go down and you don't get back up.

That was it for me. I didn't want to do a drug where blacking out is something that just *happens*. It also dawned on me that Kieffer didn't love me. He didn't even care enough about me to make sure I hadn't overdosed. He didn't care about me at all. He cared about his next high, and he wouldn't compromise it by making sure I was still alive.

I had enough. Nearly dying scared the shit out of me. I left him there and checked into a hospital in New Jersey for detox. I told them everything, all about the heroin and how I had blacked out. I was ready to get off the junk. They kept me for a little bit, but soon it was time to go home.

I couldn't go back to Kieffer. That wasn't home. I needed out of this madness, but that brought me back to the fact that I had abandoned everyone in my life. Who would help me? I ended up calling the last person in the world I expected to talk to, or expected would help me.

My mother.

For all of our problems, I owe her for what she did that day. I called her and told her what kind of trouble I was in, and how I needed help. I knew if I stayed in New Jersey I would die. Kieffer might have been used to that kind of lifestyle, but I wasn't. I couldn't handle it. My mother understood. She came all the way to New Jersey to fetch me and my meager possessions. She picked me up, then called Kieffer to tell him to have my things packed and on the curb because she wasn't letting me go back into that house. We picked up what little I owned and went home.

While it is true you can never go home again, you can visit from time to time.

I made the decision not to go to another rehab clinic or hospital. My mother tried to talk me out of it, but I decided I could quit cold turkey. Turns out I could, though it would prove hard to stay off it cold turkey. My mother reluctantly agreed to watch over me and help me get clean. I would spend the next week on my mother's couch, detoxing from heroin.

The best way to describe it is like having the worst case of the flu you have ever had, times ten. I was so sick. It was nonstop vomiting and other unpleasant deeds. Fevers, hallucinations, and just general feeling like shit. After a week, it ebbed and I was back on my feet, barely, but there. After another week, I started getting my strength back, and a week after that I was feeling better.

Life was back on track. I was home again, so I saw my son regularly. My mother still screamed at me, but at least she wasn't choking the life out of me or getting me hooked on deadly drugs. I felt good. About myself and about life.

Just in time to fuck it all up again.

UGH

12/09/12

My stomach hurts! Living in a moldy ass trailer w/ mice + roaches. I wish I wasn't living in this situation. I want my own little family in a nice place to live, not here. I got married to Courtland so now I'm Mrs. Rogers. Life is so stressful for me @ the moment. No one likes me, my husband will never trust me, and my family won't help me. I don't know what I'm going to do. We need to move out. I have no money and I'm not use to this. I've been working online but it's so hard to make ends meet + especially when everyone thinks you're on heroin and going to steal or be strung out if I live with them. I regret doing this fucking MTV show. No one will ever look

@ me the same way and I may never get my son/life back. Can't sleep, so tired I'm sick of everyone thinking I'm rich & have money because I don't. Bothers me that I'm preg. & Courtland said really hurtful things to me and I don't know if we should still be together. I thought best friends/lovers are suppose to protect you, give you attention and care about their child, not put me down. He tries to invite all his family to live with us to "help" them but if they got kicked out it was for a reason.... no offense. But now I'm a "whore, and this baby isn't his, fuck me & the baby, you play me, use me, etc." He is always making me look bad... to our landlord, my mom, his family, etc. Fuck it now I'M DONE!

Jennifer Green

This final entry is appropriately emblazoned with a huge UGH. Ugh, indeed. Things went south pretty quickly for me. I had a handle on a better life. Then from the end of September to the beginning of December, I somehow ended up married and on heroin and pregnant again.

Don't worry; when I found out I was pregnant, I quit the heroin.

It all started on my way back from Jersey. I got a message out of the blue from an old friend named Courtland, asking me how things were. We had known each other since we were about fourteen. We had never dated or anything; we were just friends. I started messaging him in return, and he messaged me all throughout my detoxing. I didn't tell him I was coming off heroin. It was nice to have someone to talk to about the good old days. He said he was in Colorado visiting his family and would come and see me soon. I liked the sound of that.

Once I was clean and could face the light of day without vomiting, I agreed to go on a date with Courtland. We met and hung out for the day. I had a craving for a fix, and decided I would go back to smoking weed, since I never blacked out from a joint before! Courtland said he knew a dealer and took me to the guy. That should've been a huge red flag for me, but I didn't see it at the time. I was blinded by my need for a high, and once again the need for some attention.

208

The dealer Courtland took me to ended up trying to sell us some bags of heroin too. I said no way, but to my surprise, Courtland said yes, and bought two. I was shocked. He didn't look like he used heroin. He was nothing like Kieffer and his crew. Courtland said he only took it on special occasions, like tonight. I thought that sounded kind of sweet. We went back to my place—I was out of my mom's house by then—where he broke the powder up on the table and did it right there. He invited me to take a hit, and I couldn't say no. I was weak and gave in to the temptation. I was strong enough to turn down the purchase, but with it laid out right in front of me, I couldn't help myself. I took the heroin and sank to that low, low place again.

It was a hard relapse. I took more than I did before. I also learned that Courtland wasn't in Colorado visiting family. He had been in rehab for the very drug we were doing, and had signed himself out to come and hang with me. We started dating in October, and moved in together by November. Courtland was not only taking heroin, he started dealing it too. The money was good but not good enough to get us a nice place to live. I hated our trailer. I started to hate my life once more.

The track marks returned, and with them I lost my friends and family. Again. Druggy, junkie, abuser. That's how they saw me. I was blocked off from my son. My money began to evaporate from my bank account. I was broke, strung out, and desperate for both a hit and just plain old love. Courtland solved this problem neatly for me by convincing me to marry him. We married at the beginning of December. So there I was, a twenty-year-old junkie living in a trailer married to a drug dealer.

What a fine time to get pregnant.

When I found out I was with child, I immediately stopped doing drugs. I might be careless with my own life, but I wouldn't poison my baby. Courtland had no plans on stopping. He kept shooting up and selling the stuff. He also became verbally abusive. His favorite thing to do during arguments was tell me that our child wasn't his because I was a whore. I cried myself to sleep almost every night. It was a living nightmare.

It would only get worse.

Off the Script

Wow. That's a lot of drama for one short lifetime. Could there possibly be more? Yes. Yes, there is. In truth, I planned on only discussing my diary entries for this book, but as I get to the end of my Zebra Diary I see that I am leaving a lot of the story hanging. So, I want to clear up a few more details before we say goodbye, my friend.

A lot of what happened between that last entry and now can be seen on the series *Teen Mom 2*. I won't bore you with the same old rehash. What I want to talk about are the in-between details. The things you may not know. I also want to go over that list I wrote in rehab. Remember the one I hinted at?

Back to me and Courtland first.

We left off in December of 2012 with me pregnant and living in a trailer married to a verbally abusive drug dealer. By January, Courtland went from verbally abusive to physically abusive. The troubles started when I was talking with a friend of mine online. He was a good friend of mine. Not a lover. Just a friend. He hadn't seen me around in a while and was just writing to check on me. Courtland didn't believe me when I told him that. He saw the messages from another man and went ballistic.

Courtland slapped me around a few times, then started punching me in the gut. By some stroke of luck, I still had my phone in my hand when Courtland started hitting me. I dialed my friend, who answered even though he wasn't expecting a call. He heard my screams and immediately called the police. When the police arrived, I worried they would find heroin at our place.

Even though I was off of the drug, I didn't want the network to know I had relapsed earlier. I panicked and sent the cops away. Then I packed a bag and went to spend the night with my mother. I woke the next morning to a pool of blood between my legs. My mother rushed me to the emergency room, where they explained to me that I had suffered a miscarriage due to my recent altercation with Courtland.

I got lots of documentation from the hospital, then filed charges against Courtland. He was charged with assault and battery of an unborn child. I decided I wanted to get out of the area for a while, to get away from him. A friend of mine in Jacksonville agreed to let me move in with her for a bit, so I got my things from Courtland and moved. Well, I wish it had been that easy.

I called Courtland and asked him to let me into the storage unit, because only he knew the combination to the lock. He met me there, and I was able to get some of my things and get out of town for a while. I thought things would settle down for me at least for a little while. Along the way, I began to bleed even more, and ended up having to have a D&C done. It was a rough time for me.

Jacksonville was probably not the best of places to go to seek solace. I didn't think about it at the time, but guess who lives in Jacksonville? That's right, Gary. Ugh. What was I thinking? Maybe part of me was trying to run from one man to another. Maybe part of me needs a good talking to! Gary tried to get in touch with me and I agreed to go out with him to see how he was doing. It didn't take long for me to remember why I quit Gary.

I had to get out of Jacksonville to get away from him. With nowhere else to go, I went home again. Courtland contacted me and claimed he was a changed man. He said he had given up the drugs and drink and wasn't even selling anymore. He begged me for a second chance. Like a fool, I gave it to him. I always give the toxic people in my life a million chances. Chances to hurt me. Chances to shame me. Chances to break my heart.

In this case, it would be another chance to assault me. And another chance to get arrested.

By April of 2013 we were back together and living in his mother's house. Courtland said he had quit the drugs, but I knew I couldn't believe him. I couldn't trust him with anything. For example, I ended up needing some dental surgery done, and had a prescription for Percocet. By the time my surgery rolled around, my entire bottle was empty. I suspected Courtland had snorted them all.

I was on the phone with my mother when I discovered this, so I asked her to call the police. Not because I was going to try to have him arrested, but because I knew when I confronted him about it, he would go crazy. Which he did. I showed him the bottle and asked him where the pills went. As expected, he attacked me, throwing punches and grabbing at me. This time I was prepared, and quicker than him. I ran around, letting him lumber around the house trying to catch me. I was too fast for him. I told him the cops were coming so he better calm down.

While the cops were there they decided to search my car. I let them. I didn't have anything to hide. Well, fuck me, Courtland had plenty to hide. And he hid all of it in my fucking car! The police found all kinds of drug paraphernalia, including some heroin, and a shit ton of money. Oh crap. They arrested both of us, of course, putting us in separate patrol cars. I knew the officer who rode with me, and I begged him for help. He said he understood and would talk to the magistrate for me. In the end, I still got charged with heroin possession and trafficking, but they set my bond far lower than Courtland's.

Two days later my world came to a screeching halt. I went to the ER because I had really bad bronchitis and had trouble breathing. While they were treating me, they asked how far along I was. I almost didn't understand the question. They were asking how far along I was in my pregnancy. I was pregnant, with that crazy, drug-dealing, abusive man's child.

A lot of you know where this is going. I decided not to have the baby. Instead, I had an abortion. I know people judge me harshly for my choice. If you are hoping for a long, detailed description of what I was going through at the time of my decision, I hate to disappoint you. I am not going to talk about my decision to have an abortion here. I have talked about it enough. I did what was best for my body at that time, and I have moved on from it.

Life moves on, and so do we.

I stayed with my mother for a couple of months, trying to get my life back on track. By June 2013 I met another man, Nathan. He would soon become the father of my second child. Most of that is detailed in the *Teen Mom 2* series, so I will only talk about the highlights here. I met him on Tinder, the dating website. He was one of my longer relationships, about a year and a half. We started out good together, just like all of my relationships do. He stood beside me when my possession and trafficking case went to court. Thankfully, Courtland confessed that all of the paraphernalia was his, and all of the charges against me were dropped.

I got pregnant with my second child by September. Nathan and I were so happy together, even if we bickered occasionally. This bickering started to turn into arguments, and soon we were fighting all of the time. I was even arrested once because we fought so damned much.

We had been arguing that day and I ended up locking him out of the house because he was getting more and more aggressive with me. I told him I would let him in after he calmed down. He ended up calling the cops, who helped him break into the house. Meanwhile, I was taking a bath (something I would learn was a nervous habit for me) and the cops demanded I open the bathroom door. I explained I was naked, but they said they would break down the door. I was on the phone with my mother, who said to just ignore the police. I ended up telling them to leave, that I was planning on packing some things and going to spend the night with my mother. They left, but returned later to make sure I was leaving. I got mad and eventually told them to just fucking arrest me. So, they did. I was arrested outside of my own house for breach of the peace. Can you believe that?

Our son, Kaiser, was born June 29, 2014. That brought us together for a bit. He was so happy to be a dad again. (He had a daughter already.) At least, I thought he was happy to be the father of my child.

What I didn't know was he had been cheating pretty steadily on me. He would text other girls and send them pics and things from his phone while he was talking to me or, even worse, he was out doing family stuff with Kaiser and me. The hard part of this is when I found out, I put up with it because I had come to expect that every man cheated. It was just a way of life for me now. Your man, husband, boyfriend was going to have a wandering eye. It's just the way men were built. Ain't that some bullshit? I know that now, but then I was too far in love and had too little self-esteem to care what he did with other girls.

He was abusive on occasion. I know; I put up with that too. I was getting used to the abuse. It was just another thing that men did. He drank a lot too. I honestly don't know what I saw in him when we met. As time went by I realized we had nothing in common.

We eventually got engaged, but even as we went through the motions of the thing, we knew we would never get married. It was never going to work. All we ever did was fight anymore. Every day was a constant barrage of hateful slurs and screaming matches. What kind of marriage is that? I can get that kind of treatment from my mom, I don't need it in a husband!

By February of 2015 we were done. He got his own place because he "needed some space" from me. That and he was fucking a girl on the side. I asked him straight up about it when he moved out, and he denied it. I suspected he had a steady girlfriend, and I wanted to see who she was. I asked him to pick up our son from daycare. I parked across the street and watched him pull up with his new girl in the car. When he parked, I had my friend park behind him to block him in and got out and confronted him.

That was it for me. I was done with Nathan for good. We got into a few more legal battles, which I will go over here in a moment when I talk about my arrest record.

I lived by myself for a couple of months. I wasn't in any kind of rush to jump back into another relationship. I didn't care if I ever dated again. I had my two sons and I was pleased just being by myself. In August I decided to move to Wilmington, North Carolina. I logged back into Tinder and met a few different guys. I went on two dates, both of which were flops. I wasn't sure I wanted to try again, but I decided to give it one more go. One of the guys I had been talking to was a man named David.

Third time, as they say, was a charm.

We met in person in September, and hit it off right away. We went out with other friends first, getting to know each other in the company of other people. I didn't want to jump right into a man's arms or into his bed. I wanted to take this one slow. If it was worth my time, I would know. David wasn't in a rush either. We finally started to go on dates together, and got closer and more used to each other. By the beginning of the year we were officially seeing each other and moved in together.

In 2016, we found out we were going to have a child. I was both worried and excited. I loved David so much, but I had also been down this road before. When I told him, he was ecstatic. He had a daughter and was glad to be a father again. He was so different from the other men I had been with. He didn't hit me. He didn't yell at me. He didn't do drugs or cheat on me. I finally snagged a good man.

I gave birth to our daughter in January of 2017. We named her Ensley. He was with me during the birth, and was so supportive during the whole thing. I had never experienced that before. It was nice to have someone who actually cared about me for once. A few weeks after she was born, David made arrangements for childcare and took me for a brief getaway from the stress of being a mom. It was all his idea. We went up into the mountains of Boone, North Carolina.

We stayed a few days, exploring the local shops and towns. One afternoon David told me to get dressed up for lunch because he was taking me somewhere fancy. That somewhere fancy ended up being a short hike up a mountain ridge. When we arrived, roses were laid out on the rock face at our feet.

"Isn't it beautiful?" he asked.

"Yes," I said, unsure what all of the roses were about.

That's when he got on one knee, pulled a ring from his jacket pocket, and asked me to be his wife. Of course, I said yes! Turns out, the crew from MTV were there filming the whole while. The thing is, I thought the roses were from an earlier memorial service, and it wasn't until he dropped on one knee that I realized they were meant for me!

The sweet part about all of this—aside from the roses and mountainside proposal—was that he made a point to make sure I was dressed nicely and had put my makeup on before we were caught on film. He didn't do this because he wanted to make sure I appeared a certain way to impress other people. He did this because he knows I don't like to be caught on camera unless I am prepared for it. So he suggested I dress like I would for a fancy meal, which was his way of tricking me into getting my own self ready for the camera. Isn't that sweet?

I think this one might be a keeper.

The List

This list falls in the Zebra Diary between the entries of May and November of 2011. It was the last thing I wrote before I left the Malibu Horizons rehab facility. It was meant to be a list of realizations I had about being bipolar. Later, I would learn that I was not bipolar. Instead I suffer from anxiety and Post Traumatic Stress Disorder from past abusive relationships. While I appreciate the diagnosis from the now defunct rehab facility, I believe the diagnosis of anxiety and PTSD fits my symptoms far better. Either way, I wrote down nearly six pages of faults I found within myself, be they the result of a disorder, poor upbringing, lack of self-esteem, or whatever.

As we go over each page, I will try to touch on as many entries as possible, but not all of them. Most are self-explanatory. I think you will find that most of them are things you probably do too. They are common problems most of us have, I just wrote mine down.

06-02-11

Sub-consiencly

Realizations of My Bi-Polar Disorder:

- taking lots of baths when bored or upset
- talking a lot and getting overly excited when topics come up such as fighting, anger, arguements, etc dark things excite me and get my adreline pumping.
- saying hurtful things to the people I love most.
- eating junk food to be happy.
- my happiness at the highest point gives me a "high" feeling.
- racing thoughts, mostly dark and drery.
- my depressive moods give me a certain high as well.
- going on spending-sprees
- started out overly happy, then over the years getting more and more unhappy and rage
- breaking point: fighting a girl over a stupid reason

and never got into a fight before
in my life and cried for doing
it for days afterwards.
- started abusing my boyfriend
and frequently punching him in
his face after the fight I had
- addicted to drama like
gossip and it gives me that
"High"
- had no idea about the happy
and extreme "highs" until
reading "The Unquiet Mind"
- thought bi-polar disorder was
about the normal level and
depressed lows but realized its
about the happy highs and
lows.
- spending money on stupid shit
and end up never using it or
throwing it away.
↑ been working on it ↑
- bought Jace 15 $5 shirts
for the summer even though
he doesn't need them
- when I go shopping I don't
try things on. I pick up

You can see here where I talk about taking too many baths. I still take several baths a day if I get upset or depressed. It's a form of release for me, a place of calm I can go to get over things.

I reflect for a bit about my first fight, which lead to my second arrest. To this day, I still feel sick about what happened between us. I never wanted to get into a fight with her, but in the heat of the moment things happen. Things we often regret. I remember when I first saw the fight video online. I was shocked at how I lashed out at that girl. It embarrassed me and made me feel physically ill. I don't usually lash out like that. I yell, but I try not to use my fists.

In therapy, I discovered that being bipolar wasn't about how you felt all of the time versus how depressed you became. It was about highs and lows. Even though I ended up not being truly bipolar, I talk a lot about highs and lows in this list. I think everyone goes through those cycles. During my therapy, I focused on the things that triggered highs in me versus things that triggered lows. I found my highs came from drama and gossip. Which ironically lead to my lows as well. In the end, my new therapist said that my highs were different from a traditional bipolar high. I don't get excited and worked up over things, I tend to get anxious and worried.

I also found I had a tendency to go on spending sprees for no reason. I would buy Jace tons of clothes, even when he didn't need them. And I tended to buy things for other people. Little gifts to make them happy, like making everyone else happy was my job. I have since learned to curb my spending and pay my bills first. Though, admittedly, I still love a good shopping spree!

a bunch of shirts, pay for them, then off to the next store
- bought iPad when I had a laptop already
- have an obsession with new phones. within the past year I went through 8-10 phones just to excite myself of a "new thing to setup"
- fasinated to fixing people's computers and how to illegally download programs, editing programs, games, and music.
- noticed when I was happy when I was pregnant I had blonde hair, then after having Jace and my mom's custody battle I didn't care what I looked like and went to black hair, after meeting Kieffer and my life getting better I'm back to blonde hair
- when I'm depressed or unhappy I wear sweats and a T-Shirt. and throw my hair back. At other times I get all dressed

up when I'm happy and dress
up for no reason and I feel great
about myself.
- When I had black hair I dressed
in dark clothes, now recently Ive
been wearing colors and even
buying bright things.
- My thoughts are so racing, I
can't slow them down.
- When I'm @ my happy highs
I can't sit still and have to
get up to explain the story with
big hand gestures and talk
extreamly fast.
- very forgetful, hard to remember
to do simple things planned for
the next day.
- Hard to apologize to anybody
- Hard to show affection to
anyone even my close ones.
- No one can control me @ all,
I never let it happen.
- When a bad idea comes up I
know I shouldn't do it but my
"high" kicks in and I end
up doing it anyways. Probably
to feel that adreline that
makes me happy.

Here you can see where I outline the kinds of things I buy for no reason. I also talk about how I go through things like phones and computers, just for the excitement of having something new. I am always looking for the next distraction so I can focus on anything but my own life.

I talk a little, too, about my hair and clothes. I am a natural brunette. I found I had a tendency to dye my hair blonde when I was riding a high moment or was really happy. I dress in bright colors and brighten everything up around me. When I am on a low, I dye my hair black and dress down and in dark clothes. I recently decided to stop dying my hair all together. Not just to break this high-low cycle, but because dyeing your hair all of the time isn't healthy. I want my hair to be as strong and beautiful as it can. So, no more blonde- or black-haired Jenelle. I am going back to my natural color.

I mention something naive here too. I talk about how no one can ever control me at all. I won't let it happen. I wished to god I would've stuck to that sentiment. I wished I had been that strong when I got out of rehab. As you know, I wasn't that strong. I immediately went back to letting others control me. Well, not anymore. I read back on this with a smile. It may have taken longer than I thought it was going to, but I finally got there.

No one controls me now. I won't let them.

- From ages 14-17 I was addicted to sex. Didn't care who it was with or if it was unprotected until I got pregnant at 17.

- From later in my year of being 17-19 didn't have any interest in having sex period.

- Just now I'm starting to accept sex again.

- I started cheerleading in middle school and excelled and even became captian. My "highs" would make me a beast and would workout hours on end and practiced cheerleading during the summer when we didn't have it and school was out.

- Cheerleading stopped once I switched to a high school that didn't offer it. Called Early College High School. This is when my depression started.

- Used my "high" in a different way and excelled in high

school and made excellent grades. Was the first in my school to recieve an A+ on a college English paper.
- In my depressive lows I could care less about school and my grades started to get low and I would skip school or classes.
- My mom didn't help my depressive lows at all and screamed at me instead of talking it out.
- My boyfriends over the years never helped but made me have more and more depressive lows.
- As I get older I frequently get panic attacks when any sort of confrentation occurs.
- When in drepressive lows I can push and push myself to do my school work but everything I read I never understood or could comprehend. But its weird because at my "high" I excell like my GPA or IQ was off the charts.

I was a little harsh on myself here. I don't think I was really addicted to sex. I think I was addicted to love. I would do anything to keep a guy with me, so I used sex as a manipulative tool. I gave them what they wanted to get them to stay with me. I wasn't a sex addict so much as a love junkie. I still am in many ways. Thankfully, David gives me all the love I need without manipulating me in the process.

I put a lot of thought into my childhood and my fluctuation with grades in school. I loved being a cheerleader because the attention it garnered me and the power of being in charge it gave me. When I started Early College Courses, this power and attention halted. I found new focus in excelling in my classes. I always try to overdo whatever task I am involved in. I need to be the cheer squad captain. I need to be first in class. I need to be the only girl in that man's life. I obsessed about being perfect, instead of just being myself.

- According to the book love is
a strong medicine for bi-polar.
This explains why I never want
to be single or be alone because
I will get severely depressed.
- The love my mom never gave to
me made me even more depressed
and angry over the years.
- Marijuana worsens bi-polar
disorder.
- Marijuana can cause schizo.
if a person with bi-polar keep
using
- Clenching of the jaw when
I'm stressed.
- Cracked my jaw for years
causing my teeth to be unaligned
correctly.
- Medication will not work for
a person with bi-polar disorder
if smokes marijuana.

The love my mother never gave me. Wow. Only a few years later she would come to my rescue in New Jersey when no one else would help me. Yeah, we have had our problems, but maybe there is a little more love there than I cared to admit at the time. I was mad, and still am in many ways.

You can see here that I came to a lot of conclusions about weed and how it was affecting my life. I don't smoke anymore, of course, but it took a long time for me to realize I didn't need the drug anymore.

I think the biggest thing I can take away from my list is that I am just like everyone else. I have the same hang-ups, the same flaws, the same habits, and same problems. Sure, we all came about them in different ways, but we are essentially the same.

We are all flawed creatures.

We are all human.

Last Entry

L ife is a journey after all. The destination is never as important as the trip.

I have had a long, difficult voyage. Some of it has been fantastic. Some of it has been horrific. I have seen things that haunt my worst nightmares, and things that leave a smile on my face when I remember them. I have been beaten, ignored, abused, and used. I have also been loved, lifted up, pleased, and comforted.

I have traveled down a path I do not recommend anyone else follow. I have gained my self-respect the hard way. Earned my self-esteem at the end of a fist. Learned to love myself harder than I could love any joint or pill or needle. Or man, for that matter.

I am glad I got to share my story with you, and I am really glad you chose to share it with me. We had a bumpy ride, with ups and downs in a wild roller-coaster ride of a life story. I might have started off as the little girl whose daddy didn't want her. But I am not that little girl anymore. I am a strong woman with a family of my own. I star in a long-running television show. I have a fiancé who loves me. Children who adore me. And a mother who, while we still don't see eye-to-eye, at least makes my life interesting.

If I can leave you with one piece of advice, it would be this: Be fucking true to yourself. Don't let anyone control you. Ever. You are beautiful just the way you are. You do not need validation from any man or woman in your life to know this to be a fucking fact. You are strong and wonderful and full of highs and lows. And you are normal. If you cry, that is okay. If you scream and yell, that is okay too. You make mistakes sometimes, and sometimes you do amazing things. That is because you are human.

You also have a story. Go out there and find it.

I hope you read something between these lines to help you find your own story.

About the Author

Jenelle Evans first appeared in the reality television program *16 and Pregnant* and then went on to star in the follow-up series *Teen Mom 2*. She is a model and an actress, but above all else, Jenelle is a mom. Originally from Pennsylvania, she now lives in Wilmington, North Carolina, with her three children. You can keep up with Jenelle at: @PBandJenelley_1 and jenellaurenevans.com.

Tonia Brown's short stories have appeared in a variety of anthologies. She is the author of several books, including *Sundowner*, *Badass Zombie Road Trip* and the *Skin Trade* series. She lives in North Carolina with her genius husband and an ever-fluctuating number of cats. When not writing, she raises unicorns and fights crime with her husband under the code names "Dr. Weird and his sexy sidekick Butternut." You can learn more about Tonia at toniabrownauthor.com.